DEAR ALAN, DEAR HARRY

Dear Alan, Dear Harry

STEVEN HARRIS

*My letters to two of
football's biggest . . .*

1999
Published privately by the author

First published in Great Britain in 1999 by
the author, P O Box 26363;
telephone: 07957 364450; e-mail: sharnip@aol.com

Copyright © Steven Harris 1999

The right of Steven Harris to be identified as the author
of this work has been asserted by him in accordance with
the Copyright, Design and Patents Act 1988

ISBN 0 9536225 0 9

Printed in Great Britain

This book is dedicated to
Mum, Dad, my family and Ella

Acknowledgements

Paolo Hewitt's advice has been invaluable. Paolo is the author of six books including *Getting High*, the best account yet of rock band Oasis. He also co-wrote with Oasis band-member Guigsy *The Greatest Footballer You Never Saw*, highlighting the life and times of one of Britain's most talented, but unquestionably its wildest footballer ever, Robin Friday, who died prematurely of a drugs' overdose aged thirty-eight. Recently Paolo travelled with Oasis on their notorious *Be Here Now* world tour. He has graphically outlined his time with the band over a six-month period in a book entitled *Forever the People – Six Months on the Road with Oasis*. He is currently editing a 60s mod anthology called *The Sharper Word*. Paolo often told me he wished to become the 'Harry Harris of his generation'. Unfortunately, after reading this book, he has had second thoughts.

All the people listed below have been really helpful and I can't thank them enough: Stella Kane, Kirsten Edwards, Jenny Tucker, Martin Ford, Laurence Watson, Simon Halfon, David Price and Barney Monohan at David Price & Co, Everyone at Dean Marsh & Co, Mark Jones and everyone at Wall of Sound, Bernie Kingsley, James Brown, Hannah Griffiths, John Armstrong, Neagel Cathcart, John Ward, The Bacon Flavoured Crisp Packet, Guy '*Calamity*' Healy, Nick Tye, Catherine Manchester, Alison Hargreaves, Chris Clunn, Steve Barrett and, of course, Claude Littner for replying to some of my letters.

Introduction

Steven Harris has been a Spurs fan for over thirty years. His first recollection of the team was in 1967, watching them with his father on TV defeating Chelsea 2-1 in the FA Cup final. From that moment onwards, he was hooked, and attended games whenever it was possible. The dream of seeing Spurs live at Wembley soon became a reality. He saw them defeat both Aston Villa and Norwich in the League Cup Final (now Worthington Cup) in 1971 and 1973 respectively. He has subsequently managed to see Spurs in all finals, including the UEFA Cup twice, as well as witnessing the highs and lows down at White Hart Lane and at many of the grounds throughout England. For years, luck was with him, watching Spurs whenever he wanted, either via the turnstiles, or, at desparate moments, succumbing to touts when it became impossible to find a 'fan' who happened to have a spare face value ticket. All seater stadia, as well as the boom in football attendances and prices during the 1990s, saw this successful set up come to an abrupt end, and as a result he was forced to become a season ticket holder four years ago. In October 1996, due to his concerns over the precarious situation at Tottenham, he began corresponding with the Spurs chairman Alan Sugar, and later with the journalist Harry Harris. This book is a record of some remarkable letters, and his somewhat futile quest to be heard.

Football is not really about winning, or goals, or saves, or supporters . . . it's about glory. It's about doing things in style, doing them with a flourish; it's about going out to beat the other lot, not waiting for them to die of boredom; it's about dreaming of the glory that the double brought.

**Danny Blanchflower, Spurs Captain,
Double Winners 1961–2**

Millions of football fans watch their team every week and don't think twice about where they're playing, or how much it costs. Football was all about Saturday afternoons. I hate the fact that it (football) now bows down to TV. I mean, who says that's their biggest earner? Every year the clubs shit on us more and more. And every time we come back for more. We're the mugs for putting up with it.

Spurs fan prior to Worthington Cup Final 1999

Q: Is TV the biggest single item of income for football clubs?

Extract from Tottenham Hotspur plc interim accounts

TOTTENHAM HOTSPUR plc

Consolidated Profit and Loss Account
for the six months ended 31st January 1999

	Note	6 months ended 31st January 1999 £'000	*6 months ended 31st January 1998 £'000*	*12 months ended 31st July 1998 £'000*
Turnover:				
Gate receipts		**12,049**	**8,885**	**14,289**
Television		**5,662**	**4.743**	**6,442**
Sponsorship		3,067	2,976	5,555
Merchandising		2,009	2,325	3,584
Other		805	674	1,319
		23,592	19,603	31,189

Tottenham Hotspur Football Club 1961–91

1961   FA Cup Winners
         1st Division League Champions

1962   FA Cup Winners

1963   Winners – European Cup Winners Cup

1967   FA Cup Winners

1971   League Cup Winners

1972   UEFA Cup Winners

1973   League Cup Winners

1974   UEFA Cup finalists

1981   FA Cup Winners

1982   FA Cup Winners
         League Cup Finalists

1984   UEFA Cup Winners

1987   FA Cup Finalists

1991   FA Cup Winners

The table shows that during this thirty year period, whilst never repeating their League success of 1961, Tottenham Hotspur Football Club managed to appear in fifteen cup finals, winning twelve.

Chapter 1

Dear Alan

It's hard to imagine now, but during 1990 Tottenham Hotspur Football Club verged on the brink of bankruptcy. If one of England's larger and more successful clubs throughout the 1960s, 1970s and 1980s (see previous table) couldn't make football pay, the financial houses that propped up the many other debt-laden football clubs may well have begun to further scrutinise their outstanding loans to a sport which continually called on the goodwill of a few to survive. Football now faced the abyss, and it was imperative that it faced up to reality. The days of the generous benefactor, with the exception of the very few, were rapidly coming to an abrupt end and, post Hillsborough, it had become clear that economic viability, as well as safety, was essential in order to turn the national game into a profitable enterprise.

During the summer of 1991, Spurs fans, concerned at the prospect of a 'for sale' sign being erected outside the gates of White Hart Lane, received some exciting news. Terry Venables, one of England's finest coaches, and current manager of the side, had teamed up with one of Britain's outstanding commercial successes of the 1980s, self-made millionaire Alan Sugar, to take over the club. This unlikely partnership had arisen courtesy of an out-of-the-blue phone call from Sugar at the time Venables was seeking investors to assist him in mounting a takeover from former chairman Irving Scholar. Together, they hoped to form the dream ticket and restore the club to the heights of former years, both on and off the pitch.

Sugar is an intriguing character. The archetypal working class boy done good and, rumour had it, a Spurs fan from as far back as the 1950s and 1960s, he'd attended matches with his father when he was a boy. The reality of the situation was that Sugar could hardly be deemed a football fan. He hadn't been a regular visitor to White Hart Lane for many years. Furthermore, in his early days, he seemed to spend more time developing new money-making ventures than watching Tottenham. As Spurs celebrated winning the Double in 1961, Sugar was more interested in selling boiled beetroot and ginger beer at school.[1]

His desperation to escape his impoverished beginnings saw his business activities dramatically expand, so much so that in 1968 he formed Amstrad (Alan Michael Sugar Trading), selling a range of goods, from plastic covers for turntables to car aerials. His pile 'em high and sell 'em cheap approach, coupled with his ruthless attempt to undercut all known competitors, became the ethos of his set up. No surprise then that, as he ascended the corporate ladder, this brusque businessman became one of Margaret Thatcher's darling entrepreneurs.

However, Sugar's assault on the commercial world was often accompanied by a vengeful anger, attacking the establishment over inherent snobbery and complacency. His philosophy was as simplistic as much of his merchandise – the aim was, quite simply, profit. And in a speech to students at City University in 1987, Sugar perfectly summed up his overall business strategy:

> Pan Am takes good care of you.
> Marks and Spencer loves you.
> IBM says the customer is king . . .
> At Amstrad – we want your money.

1 From *The Football Business*, David Conn, Mainstream Books.

Whilst he may have professed an early allegiance to Spurs (it is also well known that Sugar's brother is a lifelong Spurs fan), the kudos in taking control of one of Britain's most prestigious football clubs represented a wonderful opportunity, even though investing in football is always fraught with a number of risks. Without question, Spurs needed financial expertise, something everyone assumed Sugar could provide.

The ingredients were all there. Although Spurs had been forced to sell their greatest playing asset, Paul Gascoigne, due to their precarious financial situation, the club still possessed some useful talent. With Venables's shrewdness in the transfer market, the potential to create a top side was a strong possibility. Spurs were also FA Cup holders and, despite their calamitous financial status, remained one of the so called 'Big 5' clubs. The attraction to players from other clubs to join one of the game's more glamorous outfits was undoubtedly still there.

*   *   *

Alan Sugar's sudden interest in Spurs may also have been prompted by another imminent development in the world of football. In 1992, the contract to show live games on TV in England was to be awarded by the recently formed FA-backed Premier League. Media mogul Rupert Murdoch had recently gone on record saying, 'Sport will be the battering ram in breaking down TV's traditional cartels.' With the TV revolution in the UK about to explode, it seemed inevitable that football would fall under closer scrutiny by TV execs. After all, which other leisure activity could consistently boast that over 2m people watched the game live every week, with substantially more watching on TV? SKY, Murdoch's ailing satellite TV company, with debts running in excess of £1.5bn, would undoubtedy be a keen bidder. Likewise ITV, who had previously shown live football. Whilst their offer was to be geared towards creating greater income for the so called 'Big

5' clubs comprising Arsenal, Manchester United, Liverpool, Everton, and Spurs, ITV realised the financial implications, particularly in terms of retaining major advertisers, of showing live football. They could also promote one thing – free football.

On 18 May 1992, the Premier League chairmen gathered at The Royal Lancaster Hotel in London to make their decision. ITV's managing director, Greg Dyke, along with executive director of football, Trevor East, aware of the importance of losing live football to SKY, submitted a higher bid than initially had been suggested, reputed to be £262m over a five year period. As East walked through the lobby of the hotel, he spotted the chairman of Tottenham Hotspur Football Club on a payphone. Alan Sugar was screaming, 'These are the figures. Take them down. You better get something done. You better get somebody down here quickly. Blow them out of the water.'[1]

Sugar later admitted that he had telephoned SKY, insisting they top ITV's bid. SKY secured live football rights for £305m over five years. It was money well spent and has proved to be a lifesaver. Later, it transpired that Sugar's phone call had not been necessary. Incredibly, a call had already been made to SKY by none other than chief executive of the Premier League, Rick Parry, and now managing director of Liverpool FC. The lure of pay-per-view TV from the chief executive of SKY, Sam Chisolm[2] had obviously been too much of a temptation for Parry. Of the current 22 Premier League clubs, all of the Big 5, except for Spurs, voted for ITV's offer. Two other clubs, Leeds and Aston Villa, also voted for ITV, and two clubs abstained. But 13 other clubs voted for SKY, as well as Spurs, meaning that Sugar's vote

1 From *The Football Business*,David Conn, Mainstream Books
2 Sam Chisolm was recently appointed board member of THFC plc. Having also been appointed as an adviser to the Premier League, he was subsequently asked to resign in what was described as a potential conflict of interest.

had proved to be crucial in the satellite company obtaining the necessary two thirds majority required under voting rules. An outraged Dyke attempted to take the Premier League to court for breach of confidence by Parry and Sugar. However, the case was dropped. One further point – in 1988 Rupert Murdoch negotiated a deal to have receiving dishes made for his planned satellite TV station, SKY TV. The head of the manufacturing company – Alan Sugar

*   *   *

Sugar had played a fundamental role in one of the most radical alterations to football coverage in the UK. Meanwhile, down at White Hart Lane, his and Venables's successful takeover bid, despite a rival offer from miscreant Robert Maxwell, meant that he was now regarded as part of the saviour package. He and Venables became the darlings of the football world, often courted by the media. But, by May 1993, Venables was gone, sacked by Sugar in a bitter legal war that still rages on today. The fans were not happy. Venables was their hero, guiding what could only have been described as a mediocre team, with the exception of Gascoigne and Gary Lineker, to an FA Cup victory, and beating a formidable Arsenal side en route to the final. Sugar was often berated and abused outside the courtroom by a hardcore of Spurs fans who felt that the sacking of Venables, one of Europe's most respected football coaches, meant that yet another opportunity to build a team to compete with the likes of Manchester United, Liverpool, and of course, deadly rivals Arsenal, had slipped through their fingers.

Sugar needed to act quickly, and by June 1993 had pulled off a masterstroke by employing the services of one of the club's finest-ever players. Despite a somewhat chequered managerial career, Ossie Ardiles had been responsible for assembling a highly respected Swindon Town team, renowned for its attrac-

tive footballing style, and which eventually found its way to the
premiership (job finished by the very fortunate Glenn Hoddle).
He wasn't even blamed by fans for lack of results during a trying
tenure at Newcastle, where he was eventually sacked by an
unsupporting board of directors. Most importantly, Ardiles was
a highly intelligent, eloquent man, who loved Spurs and was still
a renowned world figure in the game. He fitted the bill as
manager of Spurs perfectly.

1993/94 became 'a season of consolidation', Spurs winning
only four home games. But before the 1994/95 season, Sugar set
about restoring the fans' faith by backing Ardiles in the transfer
market. Players such as Gica Popescu and Ilie Dumitrescu,
unquestionably stars of Romania's most succesful World Cup
campaign at USA '94, soon arrived, together with the *piece de
resistance,* Jurgen Klinsmann, one of the world's most feared
strikers, who was signed on board Sugar's Monte Carlo boat. It
was this signing that sent a clear message – Sugar could compete
with the best in the football world. Spurs had retained their place
amongst football's big guns, and Ardiles now had in place a side
comprising attack minded, high quality, flair players. The press
even adopted a name for the team's forward line – 'the famous
5'. Sponsors clamoured to become associated with Spurs, resulting in the club soon being able to negotiate one of the biggest
corporate sponsorship deals ever with Hewlett Packard, the
world renowned IT company and internet leader – a somewhat
ironic choice from the chief of Amstrad.

Unfortunately, whilst Spurs soon became one of the biggest
draws in town, the ideals of Ardiles' team – to play attractive,
attacking football – soon degenerated into farce. Spurs may well
have been able to score goals, but often seemed to allow their
opponents to score just as freely. The signs were evident in the
opening league game – a 4-3 away victory against Sheffield Wednesday, as well as a 6-3 victory at 2nd division Watford in the Coca

Cola Cup. It was all exciting stuff but didn't prevent people wondering how Spurs would fare against quality Premiership opposition. Sure enough, the cracks began to open. The team began to slide down the league table, and finally Ardiles's luck ran out when the team pathetically capitulated to 1st Division relegation candidates, Notts County, in the Coca Cola Cup, losing 3-0. Ardiles was subsequently relieved of his duties on 1 November 1994.

One of Ardiles's problems, it seems, was his failure to recognise that the team had fundamental defensive frailties. It didn't take a rocket scientist to work out that the inclusion of a hard working defensive midfielder such as David Howells could make a difference. Sugar also needed to act to restore the club's credibility, and eventually, on 15 November, he appointed the highly rated Gerry Francis to take control of team affairs. Francis, often touted as a future England manager, had proved a success in his two previous managerial roles at Bristol Rovers and QPR, seemingly getting the best out of journeymen and youth team products alike. He had a knack of buying players from lower league clubs, and subsequently realising untapped potential. Could he now work his magic at one of the game's bigger outfits?

Within a short space of time, Francis made a number of tactical changes – in essence Howells was in, Dumitrescu was out, and the team began to play a more direct style of football, as opposed to the purity initially instilled by Ardiles. Whilst Spurs became a little more pragmatic in their approach, the results were impressive. The team climbed the league, and put together an exciting run in the FA Cup, including a memorable victory over Liverpool at Anfield, to take their place in the semi finals against Everton.

It was then that the first seeds of doubt began to set in. Firstly, it was reported that Klinsmann's two year contract had 'a get-out clause', something fans initially knew nothing about. And the highly rated attacking midfielder Nick Barmby revealed that his wife had appparently become restless living in London and wished to return to the Humberside area. Whilst the team had ground out a number of 1-0 victories, it was hardly awe-inspiring stuff. It soon became clear that European qualification would be a major factor in Klinsmann staying, and if Klinsmann was at Spurs, other top quality players may have been tempted to join.

Everton trounced Spurs 4-1 in the FA Cup semi final. Spurs also missed out on qualification for the UEFA Cup due to finishing 8th in the league. Finally, Klinsmann announced that he would be leaving – for £1.35m, some £600,000 less than he had been bought for one year earlier.

Barmby soon followed, sold to the Humberside district of Middlesborough for a reputed £5.25m. Then Popescu to Barcelona for £3.3m. And eventually Dumitrescu to West Ham for £1.5m. In their place, Francis bought the following players – Ruel Fox for £4.2m, Chris Armstrong for £4m, Clive Wilson on a free transfer, and Andy Sinton at a later date for £1.5m. In simple terms, Spurs had sold four international players for over £11m, and bought 4 players for a total of £9.7m, only one of which (Andy Sinton) had briefly graced the international scene. Spurs were in credit to the tune of approximately £1.5m.

Sugar, obviously hurt over Klinsmann's departure, began criticising the player in the press and on TV for not honouring 'the spirit of the agreement'. In fact, the belligerent Sugar furthered his reputation for uncouth behaviour by hurling Klinsmann's shirt (a present from the player after his final game for the club) in disgust during an interview on *Match of the Day*. 'I wouldn't wash me car wiv it' a ranting Sugar spewed.

The fans were growing impatient following major signings by some of Spurs' biggest rivals, and the 1995/96 season turned out to be yet another 'season of consolidation', as Manchester United cleaned up in the League and FA Cup, with Aston Villa taking the honours in The Coca Cola Cup. Despite some encouraging signs, particularly the developing partnership between Teddy Sheringham and Chris Armstrong, an eighth-place finish in the league plus Cup defeats to Nottingham Forest and Coventry meant that Spurs had once again failed to qualify for Europe.

Sugar had become increasingly outspoken with his views on the game, preaching that spiralling wage demands and transfer fees would ultimately be the ruination of the game. He even resorted to criticising other clubs, particularly Arsenal, over their 'irresponsibility' when paying a reputed £7.5m for Dutchman Dennis Bergkamp. Later it transpired that lifelong Spurs fan Bergkamp had originally been offered to Spurs for a considerably smaller sum, alleged to be £5.5m. Similar stories concerning Soljskear, Zola, Berkowic, and Gullit are still in currency. With the Sky television deal of £305m over five years injecting a new-found wealth into the game, and a new five-year deal, reputed to total £670m, about to be agreed, plus ever increasing season ticket prices, Premiership football clubs were looking at healthy medium term income projections. Clubs such as Newcastle, Chelsea and Arsenal, on the back of these facts, had invested heavily in big name signings – presumably aware of the potential monies that were available not only from SKY, but from attracting regular capacity crowds, and of course European qualification.

There was no question that football's popularity was continuing to grow. It was the talk of many TV and radio shows, with an ever increasing number of fashionable celebrities suddenly making a point of pledging their allegiance to a football team. But for some reason, Sugar seemed to want to go against the grain of 'speculating to accumulate', crudely expressing doubt over the integrity of many of the foreign signings. 'These Carlos Kickaballs will milk us for all we've got, and in a couple of years they'll be off,' he said. His warnings of the potential financial collapse facing many clubs may well prove to be ultimately correct. Bigger clubs, it seems, are now clamouring to gain an ever increasing slice of football's cake by taking steps to form a no relegation, European Super League, where pay-per-view may well become the norm. But the so called big clubs need to be just that – big and successful – able to attract the best players. It remains to be seen whether Spurs can become part of this most elite of groups, rather than rely on what is now considered to be an out of date assumption that they are part of the Big 5.

The 1996/97 pre season period began with Spurs linked to numerous potential signings including Trevor Sinclair (then QPR), Fernando Couto, Ian Woan, Lee Sharpe (then Manchester United), Tim Sherwood, Marcio Santas (who at the time was alleged to be attached to Sharon Stone), Neil Ruddock, Mathias Sammer, David Hannah (Dundee Utd), Darren Eadie (Norwich), Ronny Johnsen (then Besiktas), Warren Barton, Ole Gunnar Solskjaer (pre-Manchester United), Lee Clarke (then Newcastle), Richard Rufus, Ken Monkou, Marcus Stewart (then Bristol Rovers), Ulf Kirsten (Bayer Leverkusen), Danny Dichio (then QPR), Lee Fortune-West (then Gillingham), Les Ferdinand, Slaven Bilic, Danny Griffen (St Johnstone), Emmanuel Petit (then Monaco), Darren Peacock (then Newcastle), and Jesper Blomqvist (then Gothenberg). However, actual transfer activity could only be described as thin on the ground.

*   *   *

➤   I simply couldn't understand what was going on at Spurs. Without trying to sound too arrogant about the club I support, here was a much revered (maybe even envied) organisation, which suddenly seemed to have been transformed into a club that no longer made eye catching signings, that made the rest of the football establishment stand up and take note. A club which for decades contained at least some players of such style and panache that any other football club would welcome them with open arms. Of course Spurs had some good players. But it felt like the whole kudos of the club was for some reason being undermined. Even more confusing was the fact that the man who now controlled matters at Spurs was reputed to be one of Britain's most astute operators. Increasingly concerned about Tottenham's future, I thought I'd write to Alan Sugar to ask about his visions for the future of Spurs.

August 12, 1996

Mr A. Sugar
Tottenham Hotspur Football Club
High Road
Tottenham
London N17

Dear Mr Sugar,
With the forthcoming season about to begin, I,
like probably every other Spurs fan, have been
eagerly watching the newspapers, ceefax, and
television, for any news of future signings.
  Of course rumours have been rife. I cannot
recall how many times somebody, who claims to be
'in the know', has told me that a couple of major
signings are imminent. But of course, we ask,
where are they?
  I'd be only too happy for someone to prove me
wrong and say, 'there you are, I knew we'd do
it'. However, after last season, when Spurs fans
were regularly fed with information like, 'I must
have travelled the equivalent of twice round the
world looking for the right players/ signings
will come/ a couple of quality players are in my
mind' – all supposed quotes from Gerry, I get the
distinct feeling of 'deja vu' again this season.
  Last season we were net spenders:

OUT		IN	
N. Barmby	£5.2m	C. Armstrong	£4.0m
J. Klinsmann	£1.35m	R. Fox	£4.2m
I. Dumitrescu	£1.5m	A. Sinton	£1.5m
C. Popescu	£3.3m		

  What actually happened with Klinsmann? The
papers report that he had a clause in his
contract allowing him to leave for a certain
price should Spurs fail to get into Europe the
following season. What was the point of the 'I
wouldn't wash me car with it' (his shirt)
interview on BBC TV? Surely, he had every right

to leave, especially after it was announced that Barmby was to be sold. Maybe, he couldn't see enough ambition at the club. To claim that he owed the club something for resurrecting his career is, regrettably, absolute rubbish. Mr Sugar, he was one of the world's most feared strikers before he came to White Hart Lane.

This year we have signed a guy from Tranmere . . . on a month's loan. Are we going to sign him permanently? The papers have also reported that we will be unable to use our new Danish import until Brondby are eliminated from the UEFA cup. Is this true?

Spurs fans have undoubtedly had to cope with an awful lot over the past six or seven years, but obviously, credit where credit's due, you bought a majority stake in the club, and the club has been turned around, from a financial point of view. In addition, we have one of the best managers in the game.

But what about the ambition? There used to be 'the Big 5', the five clubs with the biggest clout, from a playing, as well as financial position. We were one of them, along with Manchester United, Liverpool, Everton and, of course, Arsenal. Obviously Newcastle and Blackburn are now amongst this group. It is a shame that we are not considered in the same vein. In fact, over the last two years, we have been one of the least acquisitive clubs in the transfer market. Less active than all of the above, and less than Chelsea, Middlesborough, Leeds, Sheffield Wednesday, West Ham, Aston Villa and Coventry.

This is not some 'over emotional' fan, screaming 'get your cheque book out'. Football at the moment is very much a 'speculate to accumulate' business. The foreseeable future certainly allows clubs to be more aggressive in the transfer market, doesn't it? The new SKY deal is done, the abolition of transfer fees at the end of a player's contract. These must guarantee clubs not only more income, but save on transfer costs. Maybe ticket prices should be reduced if clubs are not spending so much, pro-rata?

I remember last year when you were accosted by two supporters in the car park, complaining about the lack of transfer activity. I remember your reaction. These people were called 'louts'. 'I've had enough', you said, 'If somebody comes up with £50m, I'll sell. I, and my family, don't need this'. Would this still be the case today? I think we as fans have a right to know.

One final question, how much money does Gerry have at his disposal?

I'd be grateful for a personal reply to my queries. I may only be a fan but, believe me, I'm as keen for Spurs to succeed as you are.

Yours sincerely,

STEVEN HARRIS

PS Bruce Rioch has just been sacked. Why? Could it be that the club were under so much pressure for success? I'd never sack our manager. I feel for Rioch, he's a good manager, but basically, Arsenal are two or three players short of a good team . . . bit like us!

Tottenham
Hotspur

748 High Road, Tottenham, London N17 0AP
Telephone: 0181-365 5000 Fax: 0181-365 5005

Mr Steven Harris

13th August, 1996

Dear Mr Harris,

I acknowledge receipt of your letter addressed to Mr Sugar and
respond on his behalf.

I think that most supporters realise that the rumours surrounding
player transfers are usually false, and even those which have a
modicum of truth may not actually be realised for a variety of
reasons.

In truth, we recognise that we do need to strengthen our squad in
some areas, and Gerry Francis has been given a large sum of money in
order to do so. We will not be spending on the scale of Newcastle
for any individual player, and regard sums in that order simply
financially irresponsible and unsustainable.

Gerry and his network of scouts have been looking on a continuous
basis for new players, but Gerry has not found what he is looking
for, and is determined NOT to spend, just for the sake of it, or pay
over the odds for the wrong player. We respect him for this.

The Klinsmann saga is 'old hat', but rest assured that Alan Sugar is
an honest and straight person, and the actions of the player were
inconsistent with the spirit of the agreement.

We have signed Allan Neilson, and he will be available to us after
22nd August.

Mr Sugar's rescue and continued involvement in the club has brought
stability and financial security. Gerry's abilities have been
brought in, so that we can realise our ambitions and challenge for
honours. The 'big 5' are NOT based on who has spent the most money
during a particular close season. Such a measure would be
ridiculous. As a matter of academic interest only, we have expended
£30m on players since 1992, and this puts us in 4th place in the
league table of 'big spenders'. Manchester United are 11th!!! I
think this proves the point (see enclosed statistics).

Your analysis of football 'at the moment', and the 'forseeable
future', are not in line with our view, and your interpretation of
Bosman may not work out that way. Similarly your analysis of, and
regard for Bruce Rioch are based on ...well nothing - a bit like the
rest of your letter.

Yours sincerely,

Claude Littner
Chief Executive

FOOTBALL & ATHLETIC CO. LTD.
MEMBERS OF FOOTBALL ASSOCIATION AND THE PREMIER LEAGUE

Claude Littner's enclosed statistics

SHEARER'S STARTS AND STRIKES			
Season	Club	Apps	Goals
1987 - 88	Southampton	5	3
1988 - 89	Southampton	10	0
1989 - 90	Southampton	35	5
1990 - 91	Southampton	48	14
1991 - 92	Southampton	60	21
1992 - 93	Blackburn	26	22
1993 - 94	Blackburn	48	34
1994 - 95	Blackburn	49	36
1995 - 96	Blackburn	47	36
Total		328	171

THE PREMIERSHIP'S BIG SPENDERS Since 1992	
Newcastle United	£59,645,000
Liverpool	£33,575,000
Blackburn Riovers	£32,873,000
Tottenham Hotspurs	£30,025,000
Middlesborough	£26,310,000
Aston Villa	£26,310,000
Sheffield Wednesday	£25,835,000
Everton	£24,240,000
Arsenal	£24,150,000
Leeds United	£20,300,000
Manchester United	£17,675,000

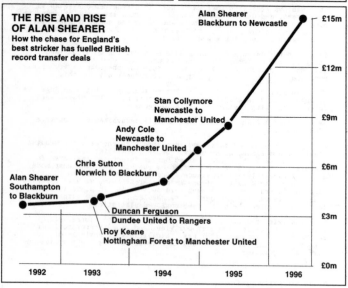

THE RISE AND RISE OF ALAN SHEARER
How the chase for England's best stricker has fuelled British record transfer deals

Alan Shearer
Blackburn to Newcastle

Stan Collymore
Newcastle to
Manchester United

Andy Cole
Newcastle to
Manchester United

Chris Sutton
Norwich to Blackburn

Alan Shearer
Southampton
to Blackburn

Duncan Ferguson
Dundee United to Rangers

Roy Keane
Nottingham Forest to Manchester United

£15m £12m £9m £6m £3m £0m

1992   1993   1994   1995   1996

➤ Claude Littner's letter clearly showed Spurs as being one of the games biggest spenders. His statistics needed further investigation.

YEAR	TRANSFER SPEND	SALES	NET SPEND
1994	£4,500,000	£4,559,000	(£59,000)
1995	£7,836,000	£3,787,000	£4,049,000
1996	£10,250,000	£11,697,000	(£1,447,000)

Spurs had actually spent £2,543,000 – an average of £850,000 per season and, unlike Manchester United, for whom Mr Littner used as a comparison in his letter when referring to amounts of money spent on new players, Spurs did not have a clutch of what were considered to be some of the most highly rated young players coming through the ranks of their youth set-up. For some reason, Spurs' highly rated youth system, set up during Terry Venables's reign at the club, was in the process of being severely pruned, some say completely dismantled.

12th August 1996

Claude Littner
Tottenham Hotspur Football Club
748 High Road
London N17 OAP

Dear Mr Littner
I acknowledge receipt of your letter dated
13th August.
  I didn't realise you were such an expert on
Bruce Rioch. It must mean that the many pundits
and fans who share my opinions on Mr Rioch must
also know . . . well nothing - I wish we had claimed
the final UEFA cup place last year.
  I am glad to see that you recognise that the
club needs to strengthen our squad and indeed I
share your comments about not buying players just
for the sake of it. I also respect Gerry for
this. But had funds have been available should he
have tried to purchase players such as Curcic,
Podborski, Fernando Nelson, Cruyff and Bergher
all individually purchased for less than 30 per
cent of Shearer's fee? What does a large sum of
money mean?
  Showing tables going back nearly five years is
'old hat'. What about the last two years? What
about the players we've sold? Five years ago
Spurs were said to have a youth team which
rivalled (some say bettered) Manchester United.
  I'm glad to see Nielson is available from this
week but what about the guy from Tranmere?
  I don't think I ever made any reference to the
'Big 5' being the clubs who've spent most during
the close season. Talk to fans from other clubs.
Spurs are no longer considered part of that club
and yet we are one of the best supported teams
away from home and White Hart Lane is often sold
out.
  As I said in my original letter I genuinely
hope that somebody will turn round and say 'told
you so' and then you won't have to deal with some

'pain in the backside supporter who won't stop
moaning'. We've got a great manager and the
Blackburn result was a great start.
  However, Mr Littner, don't dismiss supporters'
queries out of hand. Believe me I'm not alone
with my questions. We pay a lot of money to
support Spurs and there are a growing number of
fans who are becoming disillusioned with our
failure to compete with the likes of Liverpool,
Manchester United, Newcastle and, of course,
Arsenal.
  I look forward to hearing from you.
  Yours sincerely

STEVEN HARRIS

➤ At the time, I have to confess, I was a Gerry Francis fan. But as yet, I had still failed to receive any further reply from Claude Littner. I wrote to him again.

```
5th September 1996

Claude Littner
Tottenham Hotspur Football Club
748 High Road
Tottenham
London N17

Dear Mr Littner,
I refer to my recent letter, for which I would be
grateful to receive a reply.
  For convenience purposes, I enclose a further
copy.
  Whilst writing, I was interested to hear that
Fernando Couto, a player Gerry had openly
admitted he would like to sign, has in fact, now
signed for Barcelona. On Spurs club call
recently, it was stated that Spurs would not be
able to sign the player, as he would be remaining
in Portugal for at least another year.
  A similar situation arose last year over the
Chris Coleman transfer. We had supposedly offered
£3m for the player. Palace wanted £4m. He signed
for Blackburn for £2.8m.
  How come Spurs lost out again!
  Yours sincerely


  STEVEN HARRIS
```

▶ Eventually, after what was clearly some careful consideration,
Claude Littner provided me with the following response.

Tottenham Hotspur

748 High Road, Tottenham, London N17 0AP
Telephone: 0181-365 5000 Fax: 0181-365 5005

NO FURTHER COMMENT

Mr Steven Harris

13th August, 1996

Dear Mr Harris,

I acknowledge receipt of your letter addressed to Mr Sugar and respond on his behalf.

I think that most supporters realise that the rumours surrounding player transfers are usually false, and even those which have a modicum of truth may not actually be realised for a variety of reasons.

In truth, we recognise that we do need to strengthen our squad in some areas, and Gerry Francis has been given a large sum of money in order to do so. We will not be spending on the scale of Newcastle for any individual player, and regard sums in that order simply financially irresponsible and unsustainable.

Gerry and his network of scouts have been looking on a continuous basis for new players, but Gerry has not found what he is looking for, and is determined NOT to spend, just for the sake of it, or pay over the odds for the wrong player. We respect him for this.

The Klinsmann saga is 'old hat', but rest assured that Alan Sugar is an honest and straight person, and the actions of the player were inconsistent with the spirit of the agreement.

We have signed Allan Neilson, and he will be available to us after 22nd August.

Mr Sugar's rescue and continued involvement in the club has brought stability and financial security. Gerry's abilities have been brought in, so that we can realise our ambitions and challenge for honours. The 'big 5' are NOT based on who has spent the most money during a particular close season. Such a measure would be ridiculous. As a matter of academic interest only, we have expended £30m on players since 1992, and this puts us in 4th place in the league table of 'big spenders'. Manchester United are 11th!!! I think this proves the point (see enclosed statistics).

Your analysis of football 'at the moment', and the 'forseeable future', are not in line with our view, and your interpretation of Bosman may not work out that way. Similarly your analysis of, and regard for Bruce Rioch are based on ...well nothing - a bit like the rest of your letter.

Yours sincerely,

Claude Littner
Chief Executive

FOOTBALL & ATHLETIC CO. LTD.
MEMBERS OF FOOTBALL ASSOCIATION AND THE PREMIER LEAGUE

League Champions
1951 1961
League Cup Winners
1971 1973

Winners of the "Double" F.A. Cup and League Championship 1960-61
The European Cup Winners Cup 1962-63 & the U.E.F.A. Cup 1971-72 & 1983-84
Registered Office: 748 High Road, Tottenham, London N17 0AP
Registered Number: 87186 England

Winners of F.A. Cup
1901, 1921, 1961,
1962, 1967, 1981,
1982, 1991

24th September 1996

Claude Littner
Tottenham Hotspur Football Club
748 High Road
Tottenham
London N17 OAP

Dear Mr Littner,
I received your photocopied reply to my previous
letters.
  I think your attitude, and lack of answers,
confirms my, and many other fans' thoughts about
the way the club is being run.
  For the record, more and more people are now
expressing doubts about Gerry Francis. I noted
his comments that two foreign players were trying
to be signed this week. I await this with
interest.
  Good luck against Preston.
  Yours sincerely

  STEVEN HARRIS

▶ Sugar, for some reason, never replied personally to any of
my letters, leaving the matter it seems in the hands of Mr Littner.
In February 1997, the Spurs fanzine, *Cock-a-Doodle-Do*, ran an
article entitled 'Dear Claude', where my correspondence with Mr
Littner was reproduced, along with the following letters from
other fans. Before this edition appeared, the team was lying in
9th position in the league, and had succumbed to Division 1
outfit Bolton Wanderers in the Coca Cola Cup – the score, 1-6!!

Cock-a-Doodle-Do – March/April 1997

Dear Claude

You want customer care? Sugar said at the AGM that *Claude Littner is the man to contact*. The following (genuine – we kid you not) extracts are from his responses to supporters.

October

Dear Members of the Board

l write to you as a new member of the Members Club who is sadly disappointed with the 'feeling and attitude' towards supporters. >> I do not pretend to be an expert on the way any club should be managed. >> I understand [Mr Sugar] to be a clever and successful business man. >> The Club seems to be lacking any incentive to reassure its supporters that it intends to fight to [stay as] a 'top club'. >>

Having attended games as a Member and a Non-Member I can find very little benefit in Membership as there is very little difference in the prices of tickets. >> Why is the Club finding it so difficult to produce a 'Premiership Team'. With the revenue of ticket sales alone enough money must be generated to compete with bigger clubs in the buying market. Where is all the money going?

Yours sincerely

Miss B

Dear Miss B

I acknowledge receipt of your letter and though you do not specifically request a response your comments are so way off the mark that I resisted the temptation to bin your letter (after having digested the contents).

In the first place you should not underestimate the commitment of Mr Sugar. He did 'rescue' the club put HIS personal money into the club when no one else would and has since restored the financial and administrative side of the Club to its full current potential.>>

To suggest that we lack incentive . . . etc is just such absolute stupidity as not to be credible,

If you see no benefit in being a 'Member' don't rejoin. We have in excess of 33,000 Members who return year after year and who have nothing but praise for the department and the advantages which the very modest price of membership offers.

>> Yours sincerely

November
Dear Mr Littner,
'Sorry, but 6-1 to Bolton was the straw that broke the camel's back. >> I thought things couldn't get worse .>> If Spurs are going to have any chance of pulling themselves out of the current crisis they need to buy big and buy fast, otherwise we will see the over inflated ticket prices come down, not because the fat cat bosses see rationality, but because we will be playing in Division One. >> Every week we hear that [Gerry] has been unsuccessful in signing another player. Why do good players not want to come to Spurs? >> Would it have anything to do with the unwillingness to splash out some of the shareholders' lovely lolly on decent players' wages?

Tottenham used to be a big club, a club .with pride, a club famous for its brilliant passing football. >> Sack Francis and sack the Amstrad man. Don't be misled by Sugar's endless drivel about 'if it wasn't for me WHL would be a Tesco's by now'. >> Please enlighten me with your thoughts.

Yours sincerely

Mr C, Very Disheartened Supporter

Dear Mr C,
>> The result at Bolton was disgraceful. The directors all made their way up to Bolton with great enthusiasm and expectation, and we all returned feeling sick to our stomachs. We have not recovered. I disagree with you about a crisis at the Club – nothing could be further from the truth. We are well organised throughout the Club and focused on winning.

The notion of buying 'big and fast' is just the sort of irrational and irresponsible action which we will NOT undertake.>>

It is utter and complete nonsense that 'good' players do not want to come to this Club. >> Let me explode the myth about player wages. Spurs are well known to 'look after' their players and in a competitive market place we pay at least the 'going rate' and in many cases well above.

Finally it has been my privilege to have worked for Alan Sugar for a number of years. Don't believe the CRAP written about him ... I honestly believe we are fortunate to have a man of his calibre as Chairman. He is inspirational and most helpful in so many ways with total commitment to Tottenham Hotspur.

Yours sincerely

November
Dear Mr Littner,
I wish to highlight the present state of MY football club ... the club belongs to the fans and not one man. >> It appears that the people running it do not have the same amount of passion as those paying to watch. >> I cannot remember the last time opening games were not sold out regardless of the opposition. Forecasted crowd figures have no place in football. The ground should be sold out every week. Tottenham Hotspur has always been a big club, however the chairman does not agree with this fact. >> The chairman should hold the dreams of every fan. This includes spending money on the right players. I do not believe ... that Alan Shearer was worth £15m but there have been several other international class players available since Euro 96 for about £4m. >>

I do not understand why you want to spend £10m on a stand at the Paxton Road end. Increasing the capacity seems pointless when we cannot fill the ground at present.

If the chairman or any other person currently running the club cannot afford to pay to match the dreams of the supporters then ... he should step aside and look for someone who is. This is a football club and NOT a business, a football club is different. >> I sat there for most of the [West Ham] game bored along with everyone else around me. I remember when we used to tear teams apart at the Lane, now we just send them to sleep.

>> I have included a copy of Cock-a Doodle-Doo. Take some time to read this and not the Spurs Monthly. This is how must Tottenham fans feel at present.
Yours faithfully
Mr D

Dear Mr D,

>> You are clearly a passionate supporter but you make the mistake of believing that your commitment to Spurs is greater than anyone else's, and certainly above those of the Board. This is NOT the case. >> You are inaccurate in most of your statements. In the first place this is not the first time that the stadium was not full on the opening match of the season. This is regrettably often the case particularly when the match is not the first of the season (ie away tie is the opening game).>>

It is absolutely ludicrous of you to state that 'forecasting crowd figures has no place in football' and demonstrates just how completely out of touch you are. If we do not do our homework how are we supposed to forward plan or administer the match effectively. >> We need to provide the maximum facility within our budget to ensure that the stadium is full as often as possible.>>

You state that Alan Shearer is not worth £15m. How do you come to that view? You are clearly making a commercial evaluation without actually knowing anything about the business. >>

You ask why we are spending £10m on the North Stand. This is another diabolical question.>> Many supporters bemoan the fact that our stadium is not a 40,000 plus capacity. You state that 'this is a football club and NOT a business' – WAKE UP MATE Football is BIG business and if we fail to recognise that then we will very quickly go bust. >>

Finally instead of 'being bored' . . going to sleep' and generally moaning and apathetic, and writing daft letters . . . START CHEERING THE TEAM. SHOUT, SING, STAMP. . . or don't bother coming.

Yours sincerely

October
Dear Alan,
Football is a business. Who knows
that more than you? If the value of a business can be determined only from its financial performance and its share price, TH plc is doing very well and you would seem to be achieving a good return on your investment.

However, any business which lacks a vision or a strategy, and is driven only by short term goals, in a market which is rapidly evolving, will end up on its arse. And .. that is exactly what will happen to Tottenham if radical change is not forthcoming. >> The revenue stream depends on its performance on the pitch . . . on the promise of great things to come. >> Without them, attendances and merchandise sales decline, costs must he reduced (good players get sold) and the situation spirals into oblivion (a la Manchester City).

The Tottenham football team is now spiralling into oblivion. >> The very thing that made Tottenham special – its pursuit of style and flair and glory has been neutered. Not necessarily by your failure to spend bagfuls of money on Carlos Kickaballs but because we have a manager who does not have the imagination or flair to run a big football club. In short, Gerry Francis is out of his depth. >>

There's only one way to resolve this situation. Go back to business

*basics and start with vision. We
have a vision statement at Spurs.
It's over 30 years old now. >>
Danny Blanchflower wrote it: 'Football isn't about winning and losing.
It's about glory. It's about going out
there and trying to beat the opposition, not waiting for them to die of
boredom.'*

*>> Take those words and shape
your business aspiration for the
club around them – or you will see
value trickle away from your investment over the coming months and
years. >>*

*Start with a new manager – one
who can be worthy of Danny's
words. You were so close when you
began discussions with David Pleat.
>>*

*Treat the fans with a little more
respect. Get some customer care
programmes going at the ground.
People are being treated like morons
by morons at WHL these days. >>
Spurs have moved service into the
patronising 90s.*

*If this is all too confusing, sell
now. Because it will mean that you
don't understand the business like
you think you do. >> Without vision, businesses wither and die. We
don't have that vision on the pitch
any more – and we, the supporters,
are withering and dying.*

Yours etc.

Mr E

Dear Mr E,

>> I started by marking with a
yellow marker all the points
which you raised and which demonstrated a high degree of
ignorance. I have ended up with a
virtually yellow script!

Everyone is entitled to their
opinion and you have amply
voiced yours. Rather than put
your beautifully typed document
in the bin I have decided to try
and enlighten you.

No doubt you will still believe
your own prophecy and absurd
rhetoric but I will at the very least
pointed out some of the facts.

Mr Sugar put his money into
Spurs when no one else had faith
and the banks were about to fore-
close his financial return, if and
when he takes it, is therefore fully
deserved >> [But] Mr Sugar is
NOT interested in the current
value of his investment and is
FAR more interested in ensuring
that the infrastructure is firmly
established to provide the platform for Spurs to mount a serious
and sustained challenge for honours. WE are not interested in
'buying' the championship. >>
Our vision is to create a properly
financed company which will
fully support a long term highly
successful football club. If you
cannot see the RADICAL changes

both to the stadium and the 'modus operondi' which have taken place over the past few years then you must be blind. We have a strategy and if you haven't heard it you must also be deaf as Mr Sugar has exposed it at every possible opportunity.

You pour out a lot of emotional 'claptrap', but we live in the REAL WORLD. >> Try and remember where we were in the days of Ossie Ardiles!

We have had injuries and this has affected our performance – that is a fact. >> Your remarks on the youth are so far from the mark as to be laughable. >>

I have no idea why you place such faith in David Pleat. I am not saying he is anything other than a good manager but you seem to know something no one else has spotted. You continue with rubbish about treating fans with more respect!!! and customer care programmes!!! and finish the paragraph with further unsubstantiated platitudes. Your final paragraphs contain more of the some diatribe.

We will continue to do what we believe to be right for this Company and Club, and we are determined to succeed in spite of a few doom merchants.

Yours sincerely
Claude Littner
Chief Executive

➤   In view of the enlightened 'customer-care service' that Spurs now operated, it seemed that the only option left was to adopt the 'if you can't beat 'em, join 'em' approach'. I decided to write to Claude adopting his unique literary style.

February 20 1997

Claude Littner
Tottenham Hotspur Football Club
808 High Road
London N17

Hi Mr Littner,
I read a section in the current edition of Cock-
a-Doodle-Do (you should buy a copy, it's really
very good) entitled 'Dear Claude', where you have
so eloquently replied to fans complaining about
the state of the club.

Of course, these are only a small minority of
whingers, and if they don't like it, they
shouldn't come . . . oh and Mr Sugar saved the club
from oblivion by committing funds when nobody
else would!!???

Tell me Mr Littner, are you on some sort of
incentive based scheme to get up as many people's
noses as possible before the end of the season?
The more noses you get up, the greater your
reward? From your replies, it seems that the only
thing you want to get up is Mr Sugar's backside.
It was so gratifying to see that you and your
fellow directors 'were sick after Bolton, and we
have still not recovered.' I think that shows
that you care!??

The Great Bearded Wonder often reminds us that
'these mercenary Carlos Kickaballs won't be
around in a year's time.' And then he went and
bought a Norwegian and a Swiss??

Then he said, 'Klinsmann didn't enter into the
spirit of the agreement.' As you are probably
aware, Alan Sugar's worth a few quid. He doesn't
sign players with that well known legal clause,
'We'll shake hands after a pint at The Coolbury
[a well known drinking establishment in Tottenham
High Road] and this will constitute a binding
agreement.' I know this is old hat, but I love
reminding you of your involvement in one of

football's biggest cock-ups.

As you are so confident about the backing of the majority of fans, perhaps you could organise a secret ballot at a future home game, where fans can vote - Do they think you're great? or, do they think you're a tosser? It may answer all nagging doubts.

Anyway, just thought I'd let you know that the whingers are still around, and always will be, even after you and Mr S. have sold your shares at the top of the market. Happy profiteering!!

Yours kindly

STEVEN HARRIS

PS Looking forward to receiving your snotty nosed reply or perhaps no reply at all. Also looking forward to invading the pitch and demonstrating before the end of the season, and then to being banned for life from ever attending another home game, and then to having my testicles surgically removed.

➤ Spurs finished the 96/97 season in 10th place in the Premier league, and were knocked out of the FA Cup in the 3rd round by Manchester United. An estimated 6,500 fans made the trip to Old Trafford where Spurs fielded a team comprising a forward line of nineteen-year-old Neil Fenn and twenty-year-old Rory Allen. Manchester United won 2-0.

Chapter 2

Dear Harry

The letters appearing in the Spurs fanzine *Cock-a-Doodle-Do* at the beginning of the 96/97 season had left those who had experienced Claude Littner's responses in no doubt as to Alan Sugar's attitude towards fans' questions. In addition, having experienced another season of abject mediocrity, manager Gerry Francis's excuses about the underperformance of the club as a whole were becoming increasingly tiresome. At most Tottenham games there was an undeniable feeling of malaise, which the board seemed to ignore, preferring instead to brutally re-buff any criticisms.

Most football fans cannot help but be influenced by the back pages of newspapers, particularly the tabloids, with their eye-grabbing, sensationalist headlines. People seem to have enormous faith in newspapers in the UK partly because Britain prides itself on its freedom of the press, which implies that opinions can be expressed from all angles. Those without a voice should in theory be able to be heard. There seemed no alternative but to seek the assistance of a big name within the sporting press to see if the plight of the club could be highlighted. At the next home game against Nottingham Forest, I spotted just the man . . .

Harry Harris Diary note – 1 March 1997. Spurs v. Nottingham Forest

On Saturday as I watched what was, even for us, utter dross (we lost 0-1 to Notts Forest), I thought I'd try and address the problem by going to have a word with a member of the press, sitting in the next block of seats. At half time, I happened to see Harry Harris of the *Daily Mirror* standing alone. I went up to Mr Harris and asked the following question, 'Is there any chance that somebody in the press can actually write about what's really going on at this club at the moment?' To my amazement, he replied, 'Absolutely no chance', and proceeded to turn his back on me. He refused to acknowledge any more of my questions.

➤   And to think that Harry Harris is apparently known as 'the man of the people'. According to Mr Harris, his attraction in working for the *Mirror* newspaper was because he wished to 'side with the little guy against the money men . . . ' Mr Harris has supported Spurs for nearly forty years and had reported on matters relating to the club before the chairmanship of Alan Sugar. It was interesting to discover how he had built up a 'relationship' with Spurs supporters during previous seasons. Here's the proof.

Extract from THFC matchday programme dated 8 January 1992

HARRY HARRIS

Harry Harris, a journalist on the *Daily Mirror*, has lost all credibility when it comes to covering matters at White Hart Lane.

Harris, Robert Maxwell's confidante and chief supporter of his failed attempts to take over this club, used his position throughout his period to continually attack Terry Venables in his ultimately successful battle to control Spurs. Throughout, his bias was both unprofessional and obvious – and still continues.

The latest edition of the *Spur* fanzine illustrates this clearly. Harris telephoned Steve Davies, chairman of the Tottenham Independent Supporters' Association, on 22 November – weeks after Maxwell's death – in an attempt to use him and his organisation against the club.

Fortunately, his efforts to harm the improved and cherished relationship between our supporters and the new regime at White Hart Lane failed. And the revealing conversation between Harris and Davies is reprinted in detail in the *Spur*.

Harris asked if TISA were set to stage a protest – or Davies about to resign – because of the news that Gary Lineker was moving to Japan next year. 'No', said Davies, who added that the club's survival was his association's priority.

Harris then said: 'Maxwell would have been better (than Terry Venables) because he said he would keep the players,' and added 'Maxwell would have put money in.'

Davies replied: 'It's quite simple – we didn't trust Maxwell or Scholar.'

In the light of subsequent reports of hundreds of millions missing from the Maxwell companies and the problems facing Oxford United, Harris might care to explain in one of his 'exclusive' articles where the money would have come from. Would it have been taken from a pension fund? Would Tottenham now be in receivership? Would all the Spurs players now be up for sale? Would there be football at White Hart lane next season?

THFC matchday programme dated 18 January 1992

HARRY HARRIS REPLIES

The attack upon my credibility to report on Spurs' issues – as suggested in the programme for the Rumbelow Cup tie with Norwich – was both uncalled for and inaccurate.

Let me start by saying that I am a Spurs' fan and have been for thirty two years.

I worked on the local paper, the *Tottenham Weekly Herald*, for seven years, before moving to the *Evening News*, *Daily Mail* and now the *Daily Mirror*.

I collaborated with the autobiographies of Bill Nicholson, Glenn Hoddle, Terry Neil and Gary Mabbutt, as well as writing *Glory, Glory Nights*, *The History of Spurs in Europe*, *The Spurs Greats* and a book on physiotherapy with the former physio Mike Varney.

I have reported more CORRECT stories on Spurs than anyone else. Anyone who reads the *Mirror* knows that to be true.

I have nothing but the well-being of the club at heart and resent anyone who suggests otherwise.

For that reason, I helped to prompt Robert Maxwell's offer in a new share issue at a time when there were no other buyers in sight.

It was a genuine attempt on my part to aid the club in its time of need.

As for the questions of whether the money would have come from the *Mirror* pension fund . . . how should I have known that at the time or even now? Hindsight is a wonderful advantage and it seems I am being criticised for not knowing at the time what everyone knows now.

As for the conversation reported by Steve Davies upon which the attack on me is based, let me say that it is by his own admission a summary of a fifteen-minute conversation which was reduced to less than two minutes. I categorically deny I said that 'Maxwell would have been better than Terry Venables'. That is what Davies wants you to believe. Ridiculous!

I wish both Mr Sugar and Mr Venables the best of luck and hope they continue to bring success and good fortune to the club.

My sixteen-year-old son Simon is an avid Spurs supporter and

I intend to continue to report on Spurs matters and leave the public to judge its accuracy or otherwise.

I am convinced that the views of that editorial in the programme – mysteriously unsigned – are not the views of the vast majority of people inside the club.

➤   I was intrigued that Mr Harris referred to a book he had written on the subject of physiotherapy – perhaps confirming the myth that he had now truly mastered the art of manipulation.

*   *   *

The 96/97 season ended as fans had predicted. Spurs finished the league in 10th place, and Gerry Francis continued with his now ridiculed list of excuses as to why the team had not achieved any success. The season was typified when watching 'the highlights' on BBC TV, where extracts of the league table showed the team hovering between 9th and 11th place. Spurs were the only team that never got a mention throughout the whole programme. Sadly, this became something of a joke but summed things up perfectly – whilst the board had failed to recognise the reality of the situation, Spurs, it seemed, had become nobodies.

The close season saw Spurs linked with a host of top players. Once again Alan Sugar was under pressure in allowing players to be bought. To anyone who watched football regularly, it was obvious that Spurs needed to add quality to a mediocre squad. But it was almost like there was some sort of covert operation going on. Francis would intimate that Spurs were interested in signing a certain player. Rumours would abound. Then, at the last minute, nothing would happen. Nevertheless, pressure undoubtedly eased when Spurs signed David Ginola for a reputed £2.2m. Whilst Ginola has become one of the best signings for Spurs in recent times, there was caution from many pundits, press, and fans alike as to whether 'the flamboyant Frenchman' would be able to shake off his status as a luxury player.

However, what had become clear was that Spurs were not at the forefront of transfer activity at the top end of the market, apart from the smart piece of business of selling one of England's first choice centre forwards, Teddy Sheringham, aged thirty-one, to Manchester United for £3.5m, and subsequently buying Les Ferdinand, England's second choice centre forward, also aged thirty-one, for £6m. Rumours about other star names arriving at the club persisted and, given my recent run-in with Harry Harris at the Notts Forest game, I was intrigued to see whether he had entered into the spirit of transfer speculation.

SPURS IN RACE FOR £5M PAUL

PAUL GASCOIGNE is poised for a shock move back to London.

Gazza was praised by England boss Glenn Hoddle for his new found maturity after the momentous draw in Rome, where he is still an idol with the Lazio fans.

The Geordie midfield ace now wants to spend more time with his son in the capital and has not ruled out a reconciliation with wife Sheryl.

Spurs would welcome him back with open arms and he might be just the player to ignite their season.

Hoddle, when boss at Chelsea, was keen on signing him, but Stamford Bridge successor Ruud Gullit is unlikely to be interested.

Crystal Palace could not afford him, West Ham would not be his platform while it is hard to imagine he would play for Arsenal.

Therefore, a sentimental return to White Hart Lane would be his best shot.

                              Harry Harris, *Mirror*, Monday 13 October 1997

➤   This, I regret to say, was the straw which broke the camel's back. Gazza returning to White Hart Lane was about as likely as Alan Sugar replying to one of my letters.

October 13, 1997

The Editor
The Daily Mirror

BY FAX

Sir,
  Do we continually have to be bombarded with yet more
fictitious rubbish from Harry Harris about potential
transfer signings for Spurs (Gazza - 13/10)?
  Fact - Harry Harris is a personal friend/confidante
of Alan Sugar. He continually presents this supposed
upbeat analysis of the club, whilst most Spurs fans
consider the present situation to be the worst in
living memory. Even when Spurs were relegated in the
70s, people still remained loyal. Now, in a way,
most fans want Francis and Sugar to fail, because we
want them out. Sugar is without doubt on the back
foot again and so Mr Harris releases another futile
story that will undoubtedly never materialise. On
several occasions, Harris has been approached at
White Hart Lane and asked if he would write a fan's
view of the present situation. His reply - 'not a
chance!!'. Spurs fans are sick of his false dawns.
  In view of recent high profile events, public
opinion of newspapers is at an all time low. Many
people feel that the press not only lack principles
and morality but, more importantly, honesty. Surely,
it is these points that should be emphasised to
people like Mr Harris. If he wishes to write
fiction, tell him to write a book!!

  STEVEN HARRIS (no relation)

➤   I thought nothing more of the matter until the following
morning when, as I was driving along, my mobile phone rang. It
was Harry Harris. After exchanging formal pleasantries, Harry
cut to the chase . . .

Telephone conversation with Harry Harris – October 14th 1997

HH   So what makes you such a great Spurs supporter? What makes you so special? How long have you been supporting Spurs?

SH   Over twenty-five years. I think I have a pretty good idea about things at the club.

HH   Oh. Well I've been supporting Spurs for nearly forty. How old are you?

SH   Thirty-five. And what relevance does that have? What would you like me to do? Wheel out my uncle who's supported the club for over fifty years?

HH   It sounds like you're much younger. . . . someone who doesn't know what they're talking about. You know you've made some very libellous comments.

SH   My interest is simply for the benefit of the club.

HH   So tell me. You've said that on several occasions that people have approached me and asked me to write a fan's eye view.

SH   That's correct.

HH   I'd always make time to listen to a member of the public. Who were these people?

SH   I'll tell you who. It was me. I came up to you, asked you the question, and I couldn't believe it. You turned your back on me and refused to answer any of my questions.

HH   You must have looked like the sort of person who I wouldn't want to talk to. What you're saying is that these several occasions was in fact just you?

SH   No. My friend also approached you once and the same thing happened.

HH   I've written many stories over the years that have proved to be correct. If you look at the back of the Daily Record [a Mirror group newspaper] today, you'll see that they have confirmed that Gazza is coming to Spurs.

SH   Listen Mr Harris, people are just fed up of these false dawns. The club has been ruined. All these so called high profile players that we've been after. Junhino . . . we were just a pawn. We were never going to buy him and you know it.

HH   I suggest that you stop writing these sorts of letters. Do you known anything about the libel laws?

SH   A little bit, probably as much as you do.

HH   Well look. I've got your number. I've got your address. I suggest you be careful.

SH   I'm not sure what you're saying. Am I meant to be quaking in my boots or something?

Harry Harris repeated what he said and we said goodbye. The number did not come up on my mobile, so I couldn't make a note.

➤   There was a real feeling of excitement that I had spoken to someone so famous (despite Harry's attempts at a Reggie Kray impersonation) and I religiously began buying the *Mirror* to see what was going to happen next.

On 17 October, the *Mirror* ran a headline caption – 'WE'RE FIRST – SPURS IN RACE FOR £5M PAUL'. But most importantly the paper printed, 'HARRY HARRIS GETS IT RIGHT ON MONDAY'.

I was a little confused. Had Gazza joined Spurs without anyone knowing? In view of my state of mind, I subsequently decided to address the matter with Harry's editor, Des Kelly.

October 17, 1997

Des Kelly
Sports Editor
The Daily Mirror

BY FAX

Mr Kelly,
Following my letter to you earlier this week
concerning Harry Harris (copy enclosed), I
subsequently received a telephone call from Mr
Harris the following day, angrily opposing any
of the points I had made.

Mr Harris initially tried to convince me of the
Gazza story by claiming that the rumour had now
been confirmed in the Daily Record. 'Gazza is on
his way to Spurs', he said. He then asked me if
I knew anything about the libel laws, to which I
replied 'a little'. He concluded our conversation
with the words, 'Well, I've got your name and
your address'. I am still attempting to work out
the implications of this statement.

Today, I have opened The Mirror to see that in
fact Spurs are no longer buying Gazza. I also saw
(page 46) a promotion whereby The Mirror applauds
itself for being ahead of its great rival The Sun
in getting exclusive sport stories. The caption
read 'We're first – Spurs In Race for £5m Paul' –
Harry Harris gets it right on Monday.

Forgive me but shouldn't that caption have read
'Harry Harris Gets It <u>Wrong</u> on Monday'?

Whilst I have the utmost respect for The Mirror
(I wouldn't buy it if I didn't), I repeat that
Spurs supporters have had a gut full of false
dawns. If Mr Harris wants to gain some respect
amongst a growing number of Spurs fans, he could
do no worse than to write an article outlining
their opinions of the current state of the club.

STEVEN HARRIS

➤ Unfortunately, I never received a reply. In view of his strong, forthright opinions, I thought Harry may well call back for another chat. But I never heard from him. Instead, Harry delivered a masterpiece of illusion to Mirror readers entitled 'SPURS CRISIS – THE TRUTH', informing die-hard fans that 'they were their own worst enemies in trying to drive out the manager because that would leave the club in real crisis . . . Spurs could end up with a second-rate man in charge . . . ' Well at least he got something right!!

Of course, as a fan, I couldn't help wondering how other papers viewed the situation at Spurs.

. . . Alan Sugar has had his share of criticism for his Carlos Kickaball xenophobia and refusal to pay the going rate for front-rank players, but now that he has broadened his mind and loosened the purse strings, he is entitled to expect something better than two wins and six goals in 10 league games.

Significantly, despite the denial of the improve-or-else ultimatum, a Sugar-friendly columnist devoted the best part of a tabloid page on Friday to a critique which had His Master's Voice imprinted between every vitriol drenched line . . .

Sunday Times, October 19, 1997

➤ Now who could that tabloid columnist possibly have been?

EVENING STANDARD, October 22, 1997

Football dummies

TOTTENHAM chairman Alan Sugar has launched an attack on the 'dummies' of the Football Association and his own club's fickle fans.

He made his outspoken comments at the Oxford Union, where he faced an hour and half of questioning from 200 students, some wearing Spurs shirts.

On the FA he said: 'They don't have a clue what is going on in the outside world. They're out to lunch. Commercialism has completely taken them over.

'Lancaster Gate is like Madame Tussaud's. We tell our people to keep moving so we can tell them apart from the dummies.'

On the supporters, he said they were wrong to put pressure on manager Gerry Francis. 'The days are over when you could sack a manager at 5.45 on a Saturday, knowing that you had a candidate already in place by Sunday morning saying how much he loved the club,' he said.

'The problem with fans is that they apply pressure, which forces you to bring in some other idiot who is going to ruin the team more than the professional you already have in place.'

Sugar rounded on one student who had watched Sunday's 3-2 win over Sheffield Wednesday. 'Fans are so fickle that the same people who before the game had been chanting for Gerry to go were singing 'we've got our Tottenham back'. And if another couple of goals had gone in, they would have been chanting 'Gerry Francis's blue and white army'.'

Sugar also attacked some club chairman for being greedy and what he called 'the prune juice effect' of Sky TV's £150m pouring into the game at one end and straight out of the other.

'The money just ends up in the hands of agents, in inflated transfer fees and in higher players' salaries,' he said.

'Inflation in football is out of control and it will end in tears.'

Sugar also stood by an earlier promise to quit if he could not make more of a success of running Spurs.

'If I felt there was somebody who could do the job better I would stand aside,' he said.

➤   Sugar went on the attack and called fans, some of whom had watched Spurs through thick and thin for years, of all things fickle. I presumed that in keeping with his Amstrad philosophy, he still didn't have a problem accepting money from those same fickle fans. As a result, I felt I had no choice but to get out the trusty PC again and write to the *Standard*.

```
October 22, 1997

The Editor
Evening Standard

BY FAX

Sir,
When it comes to football, Alan Sugar continues to
make a fool of himself, spouting garbage at will
(Football dummies - 22/10). He may have got it right
about the FA (hardly a revolutionary statement), but
to accuse Spurs fans of a knee-jerk reaction after
witnessing nearly three years of dross, combined
with his and Gerry Francis's paltry excuses, is just
plain stupid.
  Sugar constantly seems to contradict himself. 'Fans
force you to bring in some other idiot who will ruin
the team more than the professional you already have
in place,' he says. Presumably, he refers to the
time Ossie Ardiles was replaced by Gerry Francis. He
continues, 'Inflation in football is out of control
and it will end in tears,' only months after
spending ludicrous sums of money on David Ginola and
Les Ferdinand. Surely if he had made such gross
financial miscalculations at Amstrad, the
shareholders would have booted him out.
  The time has now arrived for Sugar to stand aside
and allow someone who at least has a basic
understanding of football to run the club. It is quite
clear, the man is a prat, and he should shut up!!


  STEVEN HARRIS
```

➤   Whilst I received an acknowledgement of my letter from the *Standard*, I can only assume that my letter was consigned to the basement filing system. But I need to apologise of course to the great David Ginola.

Throughout this correspondence Harry was constantly on my mind. I didn't want him to forget our earlier telephone conversation, and wondered whether he'd now considered my earlier request . . .

October 29, 1997

Attn. Harry Harris
The Daily Mirror

BY FAX

Dear Mr Harris,
Following my letter to Des Kelly dated October
17th which I am sure you have seen, I suggested
that in order to gain respect from Spurs fans you
could do no worse than to write an article
outlining the fans' opinions of what is going on
at the club. In view of your comments during our
recent telephone conversation where you said, 'I
would always listen to any comments from any
genuine Spurs fan,' are you therefore prepared to
write the article?
    I have also noticed something. I haven't seen
you at the last two Spurs home games. And
recently, you haven't written anything about the
club. Have you given up on them?
    I await hearing from you.

    STEVEN HARRIS

➤   Still no response from Harry. Perhaps my letters were not
sufficiently exhilarating to receive a response from this world
renowned jounalist.

1 November 1997 Spurs 0 – Leeds 1

Whilst criticism for the way Alan Sugar was running Spurs grew
ever stronger from so called 'romantic' fans, Sugar could always
point to the fact that first and foremost, the club needed to run
on sound financial principals. And yet . . .

TOTTENHAM HOTSPUR have 'lost' £13.5m in the transfer market by buying players at high prices which they will not be able to recoup, according to a pioneering study by UBS.

Deals such as those involving the £6m-signing of Les Ferdinand, his £4.2m colleague Ruel Fox and the £2.6m defender John Scales have been poor value, the bank's financial analysis concludes.

Tottenham's financial director John Sedgwick dismissed the report as unfair and based on too few players. He claimed his club could recoup £6m if Ferdinand were sold.

Tottenham's purchase of Ferdinand from Newcastle United is criticised by Dr Bill Gerrard of Leeds University's business school.

Gerrard examined 1,350 transfers from 1990 to 1996 to devise a formula which rated players on age, career record and the timing of the transfer.

He said the Ferdinand and Collymore deals met the theoretical selling price to satisfy Newcastle and Liverpool and exceeded the theoretical buying prices of £4.3m and £5.5 m. 'This suggests that in both cases the selling clubs were in a strong bargaining position and able to sell the players at higher valuation.

Guardian

➤ Alan Sugar has often been referred to as a business and financial guru.

Anyway, as I opened the paper that morning, I was relieved to see that Harry was back on song. Maybe this time he had decided to write the article I had pleaded for.

. . . SUGAR HAS PROVIDED the funds for Francis, who has bought Les Ferdinand, Ruel Fox, Allan Nielsen, Chris Armstrong, Ginola, Raymon Vega, John Scales, Steffen Iversen, Dominguez and Andy Sinton.

In addition, Francis has been linked with a procession of new signings.

Sceptical Spurs fans thought that the £11m bid for Juninho was nothing more than a publicity gimmick.

But Amstrad supremo Sugar has the financial clout to have funded the deal.

In the past. Francis has targeted players like Ruud Gullit, Dennis Bergkamp and Gianfranco Zola.

It might be these three who got away that will haunt him the most if he fails to make a success at Spurs.

In Francis' defences Gullit wanted to come to English football as a sweeper. Bergkamp was a low-scoring flop with Inter Milan and no-one knew that Zola would be such an instant smash-hit.

Harry Harris, *Mirror*, November 3, 1997

➤   Oh dear! Harry was continuing to defend Sugar. However, it did mean that my relationship with him could continue, perhaps even blossom.

November 6, 1997

Attn. Harry Harris
The Daily Mirror

Dear Mr Harris,
You've gone quiet on me!!
  Whilst I am sure you may resign this letter to
the bin (perhaps even before you have read it),
I have once again felt the need to write to you in
response to your articles in Monday's Mirror (3/
11).
  Why is it that you continue to defend Alan Sugar
and Gerry Francis? A friend of mine recently posed
the question, 'Does Alan Sugar have something on
him?' 'Surely not,' I replied. However, why do you
persist with such blatant one-sided reporting?
  Did Alan Sugar really have any intention of
signing Juninho? He may have had the financial
clout to fund the deal. But he has the financial
clout to buy Alan Shearer. The point is, Spurs
fans were sceptical about this so called potential
transfer because it was yet another case of
raising people's hopes without delivering. It's
commonly known as bullshit! Regrettably, this has
happened on numerous occasions over the past few
years. People aren't stupid.
  Did Francis really target Gullit, Bergkamp, and
Zola? At that time, our chairman was continually
reminding the football world that he would never
resort to paying ridiculous transfer fees and
wages. So these players joined Chelsea and
Arsenal, and Spurs lost out. Meanwhile, this year
we bought Ginola-Ferdinand for outrageous sums of
money, and pay them £15/£20,000 per week. In
essence, Sugar had completely contradicted
himself. He recently tried to distance himself
from the Ferdinand transfer. But who signed the
cheque?
  You have written (3/11), *'Gullit wanted to come
to England as a sweeper'*. Was that the basis for
not signing one of the best players in the world?

Oh I forgot. We've got Gary Mabbutt. *'No-one knew that Zola would be such an instant smash hit'*. No-one knows whether any player will be a hit. It's such a futile statement. The same question could have been asked about Ruel Fox, Alan Nielson, Ramon Vega, and Les Ferdinand, who, as you are well aware, can hardly be considered 'hits'. *'Many believe Francis can turn it round at Spurs'*. Who are they?

Bergkamp was originally offered to Spurs for £5.5m. That's £2m less than Arsenal paid for him, and half a million less than we paid for Ferdinand. Why have you never addressed this point? Remember Inter won a European trophy whilst Bergkamp was playing for them.

During our telephone conversation on 14th October, you threatened me with a libel action for doubting the alleged story concerning Gascoigne. You said, 'If you read the back of The Daily Record you'll see that I'm correct. Gazza is on his way to Spurs'. Well . . . ???

STEVEN HARRIS

➤ OK, we all make mistakes – ref Ginola.

8 November Liverpool 4 – Spurs 0

Gerry Francis was coming under increasing pressure to resign and yet in an article entitled 'GERRY HAS TO STAY – SUGAR', Harry carried on blithely . . .

TOTTENHAM CHAIRMAN ALAN SUGAR has begged his beleaguered manager Gerry Francis to stay and help the club through its crisis.

 . . . Sugar believes that if Francis quits now Spurs, who were beaten 4-0 at Liverpool on Saturday, will be in danger of relegation.

Sugar said: 'If he makes the decision that he wants to go, I will point out that he has to go when it's right for Tottenham, not necessarily right for him. He has to be responsible.

'If he comes to me to say he has had enough, my response would be that I would understand why he wanted to leave.

'But both he and I are professionals.

'Gerry Francis is a very, very good coach and he knows what's going on, so there is no better person to put it right.'

Harry Harris, *Mirror*, November 10, 1997

➤   There were now growing rumours that Jurgen Klinsmann was going to be making a shock return to Spurs, even after he and Sugar had previously fallen out so badly.

So Harry gave it to us straight – the 'exclusive' that Klinsmann wouldn't be coming back.

Sugar 'No' to Jurgen

ALAN SUGAR yesterday killed off claims that Jurgen Klinsmann is heading back to White Hart Lane.

Klinsmann's return has been the red-hot gossip inside the Spurs dressing room as manager Gerry Francis ponders his future.

But chairman Sugar said: 'It's just nonsense. Let me spell it out once and for all. There have been no moves to bring Jurgen Klinsmann here either as a manager or as a player.'

Harry Harris, *Mirror*, 17 November 1997

➤ And in the meantime, Paul Gascoigne had actually gone on record to saying that a return to football in London was unlikely. In fact, Gazza subsequently signed for Middlesborough.

November 17, 1997

Attn. Harry Harris
The Daily Mirror

BY FAX

Dear Mr Harris,
I am sure you will have seen that at least two other leading national newspapers (Guardian and The Mail) have recently highlighted reports from experts who have questioned some of the financial dealings at Spurs. Why haven't you decided to investigate these reports?
  Ref: Your article 11/11/97 – 'even Spurs fans might believe it is better to have Francis than no manager at all'. Why? Sounds like another Sugar line.
  Ref: 'I'll Kiss Britain Goodbye' – By Mark Irwin 14/11/97 (copy enclosed) – remember our telephone conversation on 14th October 1997 where you said, 'Gazza is on his way to Spurs'?? . . . 1-0 to me!!
  Ref: Your article – Sugar 'No' to Jurgen – 17/11/97 – comments noted.
  I am still waiting to see whether you are prepared to write an article outlining the fans' opinions of what is going on at Spurs.

  STEVEN HARRIS

TOTTENHAM will today unveil Swiss unknown Christian Gross as their new head coach in a massive gamble.

The shock appointment finally marks the end of Gerry Francis's turbulent three-year reign at White Hart Lane and the club's players will be told the news at a square meeting this morning.

Harry Harris and Mark Irwin, *Mirror*, November 19, 1997

► **19 November 1997** Gerry Francis resigned and Sugar appointed Christian Gross, a foreign manager. Not a Carlos Kickaball then, but perhaps a Manuel Manag'em, or a Govan Guvnor.

Announcing Francis's departure from Spurs, Sugar, in his inimitable style, summed things up perfectly by stating, 'I believe that if Gerry came back tomorrow wearing a mask and calling himself Francisco Geraldo then he would be hailed as a saviour. His training methods and tactics would be hailed as the best and everything would turn around very quickly'. So, Sugar's rationale seemed to be that if we spent £20 on a mask, we'd start winning.

Not everyone was pleased about the appointment of Christian Gross. But the chairman defended his decision with vigour.

SUGAR BLASTS MULLERY

ALAN SUGAR said he was 'totally disgusted' by 'an irresponsible outburst' by former Tottenham favourite Alan Mullery, who criticised the appointment of Christian Gross.

Mullery said he was 'not impressed' by Gross's credentials, adding 'We could all do what he has done in Switzerland.

'He has won the Swiss championship but that is like winning the championship in Scotland.

'It is probably impressive in Switzerland, but not in England. I like their chocolate but . . . '

Mirror, 20th November

► Christian Gross took charge of his first game at home against Crystal Palace. Spurs lost 1-0. I saw Harry at the game (although he didn't know who I was), and thought I'd better re-open discussions with him about our new manager.

November 26, 1997

Harry Harris
Daily Mirror

BY FAX

Dear Harry,
Nice to see you at White Hart Lane yesterday to
witness the beginning of Gross.
  Seeing as Alan Sugar has decided to once again
contradict himself by employing a foreign coach
having originally stated in his wonderful open
minded diatribe, 'they'll milk us for all we've got
and then they'll be off', would you not agree that
should Mr Gross not be able to deliver success,
Spurs fans would have every right to blame Sugar for
poor selection? After all, Mr Gross is his third
attempt to get it right.
  How come you never got the 'exclusive' that we were
going to be signing Mr Gross? I would have thought
that Sugar would have given you the nod.
  In your article (Appliance of Soccer Science - 19/
11), you claimed that Francis passed by the chance
of signing Gullit, Bergkamp and Zola. But if you
remember, Sugar at the time said that he would 'not
get involved in these ridiculous transfer fees'. Why
don't you ever make this point? The fact was that
Sugar wasn't prepared to pay these transfer fees for
world class players. His failure to have a basic
understanding and acknowledgement of quality may
well have led to Francis buying substandard players,
and ultimately losing his job. Sugar than had the
cheek to blame the press for Francis's downfall.
  I'm still having a few restless nights trying to
work out what your comments meant ('I've got you
name, your number, and I know where you live'),
following my letter to Des Kelly on 13th October.
  Finally, is Brian Woolnough joining the Mirror?

  STEVEN HARRIS

➤   And of course, I had to write to the chairman as well. Well,
it would be rude not to.

November 26, 1997

Alan Sugar
THFC
808 High Road
Tottenham
London N17

Dear Mr Sugar,
As you are probably aware, many people's initial
response to your appointment of Christian Gross was
Christian who? Let's hope, for your benefit, that he
proves to be an inspired choice. However, whilst
Arsene Wenger's appointment at Arsenal was
immediately endorsed by none other than England
coach Glenn Hoddle, as well as former world player
of the year George Weah, the only player to have
endorsed Mr Gross's appointment was our own Ramon
Vega. In addition, Mr Wenger was given a substantial
budget to create a formidable squad. Which begs the
question, having witnessed another dire performance
against Crystal Palace, how much money, if any, does
Mr Gross have at his disposal? Or are you hoping
that Mr Gross will be able to conduct transfer
dealings in a far more prudent manner, by perhaps
disposing of some existing members of the squad in
order to buy others? Regrettably, it seems that the
team's performance against Palace was simply an
indictment of Gerry Francis's reign at Tottenham. It
does appear that we are still a long way from having
a squad that can challenge for the Premiership.
Saturday, we play Everton. Some might say, a clash
between two of the Big 5???
   In view of the enormous pressure you must now be
feeling having appointed your third manager in six
years, I wondered whether your comments last year
on national TV ('if I do not succeed within two to
three years, I'm off'), still stand?
   Looking forward to hearing from you.
   Respectfully yours

STEVEN HARRIS

➤ Surprise surprise!! No response whatsoever to this letter.

➤   Things didn't seem to be going too well for the beleaguered
chairman and soon he was put on the spot at the club's AGM.

THE MAIL November 28, 1997

You exploit our loyalty, Sugar told

Fans slam Spurs chief over slide into chaos

TOTTENHAM were yesterday accused of treating their fans with contempt and insulting their intelligence in a stormy annual meeting at White Hart Lane attended by more than 500 shareholders.

Chairman Alan Sugar and his board came under attack as one supporter announced to the packed room, 'There is one club in north London that treats its customers with respect and behaves with decorum.

'Another, also in north London, treats its fans with contempt, delivers an inferior product, invests unwisely, squanders assets, demotivates employees and claims that buying Les Ferdinand was a mistake. It also insults fans' intelligence by pushing up prices and exploiting their loyalty.

'As shareholders we must send a message to the board that things must get better.'

It was a stinging attack on Spurs' handling of events over the 1st year that culminated with the resignation of manager Gerry Francis and the appointment of Swiss coach Christian Gross to take his place.

Sugar himself took time to criticise how Francis ran the club and how things, especially the youth policy, were allowed to get out of control. He said: 'We've seen a major slide in youth development. We have to invest basically and are talking about an amount that is peanuts. We cannot go on spending £6-7m. It's madness.

'We have to begin grooming players who have the Tottenham

shirt on their shoulders from the age of 14 or 15, so we have youngsters playing for that shirt and not a four-year contract.'

In reply to a shareholder's demand that England defender Sol Campbell must not be allowed to leave White Hart Lane, Sugar replied, 'No money in the world would move him from this club'.

There has been speculation that the Spurs skipper will be the next star to walk out, disillusioned at the downward spiral which sees Spurs just one point off the Premiership's bottom three.

Sugar, speaking about Francis and his inability to stop that slide, added: 'Basically, he got into a tailspin, things got out of his control, and he could not get them back. The board just provides the money but the manager determines and instructs on the players he wants and recommends them.

'But we can no longer attract the big names to White Hart Lane. Players like Dennis Bergkamp and Jurgen Klinsmann don't wake up in the morning and say they'll come to England and decide they'll join Spurs.'

Sugar then stressed the need to bring into the club a general manager to work separately from coach Christian Gross, who did not attend the meeting so he could concentrate on his first full training session with the team.

He added: 'Contrary to what you may have been led to believe, the training ground will not be changed to Colditz camp. But I have a good feeling that Mr Gross will do well here and I have confidence to him.'

Gross last night revealed how the move has made him a millionaire.

The Swiss-born coach revealed details of his eighteen-month contract said: 'I'll be earning more than one million Swiss francs, £450,000 a season. After tax it will be a little less than a million. But I will receive bonuses on top of my basic salary.'

The package has doubled the former Zurich Grasshopper manager's earnings.

➤ Just over two weeks ago, Sugar was telling everyone 'Gerry is a very very good coach'. Now Francis was out of the picture, Sugar began laying the blame for the decline squarely at the feet of the former manager. In addition, Sugar informed us that both Klinsmann and Bergkamp 'Don't wake up in the morning and say they'll join Spurs'. Well Klinsmann did. And Bergkamp was offered to Spurs. The fact was that we (Sugar) wouldn't spend the money.

➤   And where was Harry in all of this?

```
November 28, 1999

Harry Harris
Daily Mirror

BY FAX
Dear Harry,
I notice you haven't written anything about the AGM
which took place at Spurs yesterday, where it seems
your friend Mr Sugar got what he deserved for
potentially ruining what was once a big football club.
  He even had the gall to openly criticise Francis,
having recently made his 'Geraldo Francisco' speech.
  Still waiting for some answers to some rather
searching questions.


  Steven Harris
```

➤   Having so vigorously defended his appointment of
Christian Gross, particularly against Alan Mullery, the chairman
provided a confidence boosting statement for the new manager

THE MIRROR, November 28th, 1997

Sugar: Gross was
our last resort

Alan Sugar last night admitted that Christian Gross is the new manager purely because he was the only European coach available.

The Tottenham chairman responding to criticism of the appointment of the Swiss coach at the club's stormy AGM last night said, 'We looked all around Europe for people with credentials, but it is a fact that anyone who is any good was already tied up in a job.'

➤ I'd tried the chairman, I'd tried Harry, but to no avail. I now thought I'd try and get the inside track about some of the goings on at Spurs by writing to Teddy Sheringham.

```
November 28, 1997

Teddy Sheringham
c/o Manchester United FC
Old Trafford
Manchester
M16 0RA

Dear Teddy,
I hope you believe me when I tell you that I was
not one of the Spurs fans who booed you when you
played your first game for Manchester United
earlier this season. Frankly, I was more
concerned with the fact that you had left the
club. Which leads me to the reason why I am
writing to you.
   I've heard various rumours as to why you left,
in particular that he [Sugar] accused you of
feigning injury just after you had broken into
the England squad, but wondered whether you could
shed any light on the situation.

   STEVEN HARRIS
```

➤ No luck here either, but Teddy later confirmed his run-in with Sugar in his book.

Things were critical on the pitch, the team lying in a perilous, relegation-bound position. So who better than our illustrious chairman to take it upon himself to boost team morale.

THE MIRROR, November 29, 1997

THEY'RE NOT FIT TO WEAR SPURS SHIRT

Sugar in new blast at his players

ALAN SUGAR is facing a player revolt after savaging Tottenham's superstar signings and claiming: 'They're not fit to wear the shirt on their backs'.

The outspoken Spurs chairman has laid the blame for the club's Premiership problems squarely at the feet of the players and openly questioned their commitment to the club.

Now his amazing own goal, on the eve of Christian Gross's first game in charge, is threatening to tear the club apart.

'My opinion is that the demise of the club is because of a lack of team spirit,' Sugar said.

'Certain players are lured in and believe they have a right to wear a Tottenham shirt. The problem is that some don't deserve to have it on their backs.

'They sometimes think they are more important than they are. They need knocking into shape a bit and being reminded a little more of what a privilege it is to be at this club.

'The kids who have been brought through the youth system, the Sol Campbells, the Walkers, Barmbys and Samways, play with their hearts on their sleeves.

'It's the people who are purchased, brought in as so called superstars, that need to be scrutinised over their commitment to the club.'

Criticism

Sugar was particularly scathing

about the club's overseas signings, singling out Romanian failures Ilie Dumitrescu and Gica Popescu for personal criticism.

'Under Ossie Ardiles there were five loonies bombing forward and they forgot about the ball going in at the other end. After the euphoria it was 'get your effing cheque book out and Ossie out'.

'It took a Francis style regime to come in a immediately get Dumitrescu out and bring back players that Ardiles didn't want, players like Howells, to bring some stability back.

'I think that Gerry, having had a bellyful of foreign players, made the fatal mistake of completely closing his mind to any foreign players for the next season.'

Now he blames the team Francis left behind for failing to support his latest signings, claiming: 'I've seen Ginola running around working his heart out and not being supported by his own colleagues because they believe he is there on his own agenda.

'Also Dominguez running about, again on his own agenda. They claim they don't defend and don't go back.'

His comments were met with astonishment by Danish midfielder Allan Nielsen as the team travelled north to Merseyside yesterday for the crunch clash with fellow strugglers Everton.

'It doesn't matter where a player is born,' the £1.65m mid-fielder said. 'Everybody at this club knows I will always give 100 per cent effort. That is the way I am.

'I am completely committed to Tottenham Hotspur and I don't believe they would have bought me if they had any doubts about that.'

Sugar launched his scathing attack during an address to the Cambridge University's Union Society this week and banned the press for fear that his comments would become common knowledge.

Ironically, he refused to criticise the team during Thursday's stormy AGM, insisting he wanting to encourage them for today's vital relegation battle.

He has already upset £6m-record-signing Les Ferdinand with his comments this season and now has to pick up the pieces all over again after his latest own goal.

➤ I wondered whether anyone had had the guts to tell Mr Sugar that Barmby and Samways 'play with their hearts' on their sleeves at Everton? And why did we have to sell these whole hearted 'kids' in the first place?

Everton 0 – Spurs 2

DAVID GINOLA and Ramon Vega rammed the words of Spurs' chairman Alan Sugar back down his throat to give new boss Christian Gross a perfect start in his first game in charge.

Sugar had slammed Spurs superstars in the pre-match build up, claiming: 'They're not fit to wear the shirt on their backs.'

But in a game vital for both sides, Vega and Ginola brought victory with second half goals.

Mirror, December 1st, 1997

➤   I couldn't help thinking that evening that Sugar was sitting at a dinner party smugly telling people that this result was all down to him with his pre-match psychobabble and 'prove me wrong' theory. However, comparisons with Sigmund Freud seemed a little premature.

Sugar was getting on my nerves. All the man could do was criticise everyone but himself. I decided to try my luck by writing to Goal Magazine, and much to my delight, I had some success.

Goal Magazine

Letter of the month . . .

If Alan Sugar and Gerry Francis had the courage to admit that errors of judgement had been made at Spurs, then they may at least gain some respect from the fans. Is Sugar really the great financial guru he would have us believe? The 'buy low, sell high' philosophy favoured by him seems to have been overlooked when it comes to Tottenham's transfer dealings.

Two years ago, Sugar completely missed the boat when it came to signing high quality internationals, refusing to pay the wages or transfer fees. He criticised Arsenal for buying Dennis Bergkamp – a lifelong Spurs fan – claiming exorbitant fees would ruin the game. Eighteen months ago, Eyal Berkowic was reportedly prepared to pay his own fare from Israel and sign for Spurs on a free transfer, but Sugar wasn't interested, then we go and bid £1.5m to sign him from Southampton. To think we could have had a forward line of Bergkamp, Zola (offered to Spurs before Chelsea) and Soljskaer. And still Sugar maintains the Spurs haven't been left behind!

With a bit of style injected, we could easily be attracting crowds of 40,000 – during the Klinsmann season you couldn't get a ticket for a home game. Now, we struggle to fill a ground which, when finished, will still only hold 35,000, while Arsenal need another 10,000 seats.

Where's the financial wizardry in that, Mr Sugar?

Stephen Harris, London

➤   I hadn't seen much from Harry recently, and there seemed to be early signs that he was no longer speculating about forthcoming transfers.

Spurs 1 – Chelsea 6

IT WAS A GROSS injustice. A day of shame and star quality.
The shame belonged to the Spurs players who trooped away
heads bowed, with vitriol stinging their ears from disillusioned
supporters . . .

. . . Gross dismisses suggestions that the team's plight is far
worse than he imagined when Sugar recruited him.
He has united the dressing room and that is no mean feat for a
foreign coach entering English football at a crisis club.

Harry Harris, *Mirror*, December 8th, 1997

➤   Note how Harry informed us how . . . 'Gross has re-
united the dressing room'. I wondered, was this before or after
the 6-1 drubbing? Then on the very next day, Sugar predictably
promised 'another substantial treasure chest'. Where have we
heard that before?

The more I heard about the goings on at Spurs, the more
concerned and anxious I was becoming about the state of the
club. It was time to try Harry one more time, 'Still waiting to see
whether you are able to write a fan's eye view of what's really
been going on at the club', I asked him. But my pleas went
unheard, which became a little depressing. Didn't anyone share
my views? Was I really, as Sugar had put it, 'fickle'? Thankfully,
Matthew Norman from the *Standard* put my mind at ease. In an
incisive attack on Sugar, he wrote, 'Every time he (Sugar) opens his
mouth, he makes himself look more of an ass than ever. An
astounding achievement, this, since the tails and ears were in place
the moment he uttered the imbecile words 'Carlos Kickaball'.'

Mr Norman went on, 'Consider Mr Sugar's reaction to Gerry
Francis's departure. First, he insisted that he wanted him to
stay. Gerry, he said, was still a talented coach and the best man
for the job. A few days later, Mr Sugar savaged the same Gerry
Francis at a shareholders meeting . . . Even at its peak, John

DEAR HARRY   75

Major's government seldom achieved so swift and spectacular a
self-contradiction . . . Then he turned on the fans, sneeringly
deriding their desire for 'entertainment and all that stuff'. If
there were five words which could pinpoint anyone's unfitness
to run Tottenham, Sugar found them like an Exocet . . . I
recently heard of a man who had given up his season ticket after
forty years . . . '

13 December 1997 Coventry 4 – Spurs 0

Another desperate performance from the team culminating
in defender Colin Calderwood being accused of gesturing an
obscenity towards the travelling fans.

Despite the turmoil at the club, Harry incredibly seemed
intent on defending Sugar, and so the PC was again dusted down
and aimed in his direction.

December 13, 1997

Harry Harris
The Daily Mirror

BY FAX

Dear Mr Harris,

> Tottenham Chairman Alan Sugar has put
> his money where his mouth is with vast
> investments in the transfer market – only to
> be savaged by 'experts' who have branded
> it a waste of money.
>
> Surely, it didn't need any City analyst to
> work out that £6m was over the odds for a
> 30-plus striker like Les Ferdinand. Anyone
> could have sussed out that £4.25m for Ruel
> Fox wasn't the best investment of all time.
>
> Everyone knew it, but market forces
> blackmailed Sugar into paying these prices
> against his better judgement.

Yet more claptrap in your article dated 11/12/97
(see above) – 'market forces blackmailed Sugar
into paying these prices against his better
judgement'????
Are you sure??
It seems a shame that such one-sided reporting
should appear in a reputable newspaper such as
The Mirror . . .
Yours sincerely

STEVEN HARRIS

➤ I also forgot to mention to Harry the fact that if Sugar knew that £6m was 'over the odds' for Les Ferdinand, then why the hell did he pay it? Was this so called great financial guru getting things so badly wrong??

It seems as though he was . . .

THAT NOTION may only be whispered at the moment, but it is beginning to circulate among the money men, the boys who buy and sell Spurs shares.

They have very nearly halved this year, from 138p to 77½p . . .

Another City suit was more blunt: 'Sugar hates the City, and the City will not learn to love Spurs shares while he's still there.'

Such comments met a predictably frosty response from the Sugar side. A spokesman said: 'There is no sign that Alan Sugar is beginning to think he might sell.

'It is amazing how people with a strong financial brain ignore the fundamentals as soon as they start talking about football.

'Alan Sugar is so ambitious for the club. Tottenham has very strong management, and it is very well run. This bad spell is about what happens on the pitch. That is not Sugar's area.

Mail, December 13th, 1997

➤ In response to criticism from the City, a spokesman for Sugar said, 'it's amazing how people with a strong financial brain ignore the fundamentals as soon as they talk about football.' A somewhat surprising statement from someone presiding over a twelve-month-halving of their company's share price. However, Alan Sugar is of course a renowned football expert. ('What's the double' – Alan Sugar 1991)

20 December 1997 – Harry made a welcome return to transfer speculation by informing us that Christian Gross wished to sign Lee Carsley from Derby. Lee Carsley subsequently signed for Blackburn Rovers. Presumably, the 'substantial treasure chest' was under lock and key.

The rumours were still rife concerning Jurgen Klinsmann making a shock return to Spurs. And yet . . .

ALAN SUGAR has blocked an attempt by Christian Gross to sign Jurgen Klinsmann on loan until the Summer.

The Spurs chairman scrapped the deal when he discovered Klinsmann was demanding £40,000 a week.

But Sugar was not prepared to smash his wage structure. He felt Klinsmann needed Spurs more than the club needed him.

Sun, December 20th, 1997

➤ What a shame! Alan Sugar had decided to block any move to re-sign the German maestro. And in a frank interview with the *Sun*, former manager Gerry Francis informed fans that ex Spurs hero Teddy Sheringham 'wanted to stay'. So if England's centre forward wanted to stay, then why the hell did he leave? Three days later after Sugar informed the world that Klinsmann wasnt returning to Spurs . . .

21 December 1997 Spurs 3 – Barnsley 0

JURGEN KLINSMANN will pick up close to £1m for twenty weeks' work at Tottenham and then quit the club again.

The German striker's contract at White Hart Lane runs until the end of June and then the wandering star plans to finish his career in Japan or America.

Klinsmann's salary will be in excess of £30,000 a week for just over four months in north London, where he will play only two out of twenty-six games.

But the truth behind Klinsmann's surprise return to Spurs has more to do with his desire to do well in the World Cup than a mega-money deal to save the once great North London club from the humiliation of regulation or the lure of a Wembley Final.

Tottenham chairman Alan Sugar said: 'It's perfect for both of us. He's got to play regularly at the top level'.

Harry Harris, *Mirror*, December 23rd, 1997

➤   What a shocker!! Klinsmann was back. A magnificent 'U' turn by Mr S. Everyone should be celebrating, shouldn't they?? Certainly the fans were ecstatic. He may be costing the club a lot of money, but he's a proven class act, and he may attract other big names to the club. But what's this?? Harry, for some reason, was bad-mouthing him. Peculiar. Three years previously a Jurgen Klinsmann biography appeared in all leading book shops. Writer? Mr Harold Harris.

Alan Sugar's approach to matters Klinsmann was perfectly summed up in the *Guardian*.

THE GUARDIAN, December 23rd, 1997

A word from the chairman

'This guy is special. He came to the meeting seeking a challenge, not loads of money. In my business you meet some hard dealers. He is the most genuine, honest footballer I have met'
Alan Sugar, August 1994

'I wouldn't wash my car with Klinsmann's shirt now. There you are, you can have it if you want it'
Alan Sugar, August 1995

'He really enjoyed his time here. We have solved our problems a long time ago and he really does like the club and enjoyed the way the British public treated him'
Alan Sugar, yesterday

With the festive season upon us, it was time to put all bad feelings to one side. MERRY XMAS HARRY.

Dear Harry,

With Best Wishes
for Christmas
and the coming Year

Looking forward to
some excellent news stories in
1998

Steve

JURGEN KLINSMANN quit Sampdoria for Tottenham after invok-
ing a clause in his contract that he could NEVER be dropped.

As soon as his hard line boss in Genoa, Yugoslav Vudjadin
Boskiv, dared to leave out Klinsmann, Germany's World Cup
skipper walked out to rejoin Spurs within days.

Now it is believed he has brought the same terms with him to
White Hart Lane insisting that Christian Gross will not axe him
from the first team if he suffers a slump in form . . .

                        Harry Harris, *Mirror*, 24th December 1997

➤   Harry was not entering into the Xmas spirit and continued
to question Jurgen's motive. Maybe his book on Jurgen wasn't a
best seller? Or maybe there was someone else behind Harry's
vitriol . . .

Boxing Day Aston Villa 4 – Spurs 1

28 December 1997   There now followed a shock for Claude –
he was outed in the *Sunday People*. The article explained how
Claude had managed to alienate many fans with his abrasive and
abusive letters. All of Claude's replies in *Cock-a-Doodle-Do* were
highlighted. In particular, where he accused one fan of 'a high
degree of ignorance and downright stupidity', and the time he
responded to another, 'I have no idea why you place such faith in
David Pleat' – a surprising comment in view of the fact that Pleat
had just been appointed a director of football at Spurs. The
article merely confirmed the way supporters felt they were
regarded by the board of directors. Even by Sugar's standards, it
was baffling to think that he had employed Claude to be the
public face of Spurs and deal directly with fans' complaints. Was
this really a constructive way of fulfilling a promise from an
earlier AGM where Sugar stated, 'You want customer care?' (I'll
give you customer care)?

➤   There soon followed more bad news for the board at
Spurs . . .

JURGEN KLINSMANN will receive a hero's welcome back at
White Hart Lane today from 30,000 adoring Tottenham fans.

But the man who became the German superstar's closest
friend and minder during his first sensational spell at Spurs will
not be among them.

For former Tottenham security officer Mick Southam has
been mysteriously banned from White Hart Lane and the club's
training ground.

'What's worse, my son Glenn was at Spurs' school of Excel-
lence — yet I wasn't even allowed to go and watch my own boy
play. I was told I would be ejected,' said Mr Southam.

News of the World, December 28th, 1997

➤   How can a father not be allowed to watch his own son play
football?

Arsenal 1 – Spurs 1

JURGEN KLINSMANN'S homecoming was a masterpiece of
illusion.

After all the hype, the billing as the greatest comeback since
Frank Sinatra . . . there was no escaping reality.

The German World Cup captain has returned to White Hart
Lane after two-and-a-half years' absence as much to rescue
himself as to save Spurs.

Klinsmann's hurried resumption of his Spurs career was
hardly that of a return of the prodigal son.

Instead, the 33-year-old superstar is in urgent need of
sharpening up his game or he will risk losing his World Cup
place in France.

Harry Harris, *Mirror*, December 29th, 1997

➤   Harry was still on Jurgen's back. Enough was enough. I
needed to have a word with him . . .

December 29, 1997

Harry Harris
The Daily Mirror

Dear Mr Harris,
Unfortunately, I can't help disagreeing with much
of the drivel that you continue to feed to
readers of the *Daily Mirror*.
   Instead of attempting to castigate Jurgen
Klinsmann in your article dated 24th and 29th
December, presumably as some sort of tactic to
divert flak from your mucker Mr Sugar, you should
perhaps be concentrating on why the bloke was
allowed to leave in the first place. Money
orientated Mr Klinsmann may be, but if Sugar had
any sort of foresight back in the days of his
'Carlos Kickaball' and 'car washing' comments,
he'd have broken the bank to retain Klinsmann's
services so that perhaps Spurs could have
progressed. Even if he plays badly, Klinsmann's
clout could be the only thing that attracts
quality players to the club. Presumably you're
trying to cover your back (and Sugar's) for the
time when Klinsmann will undoubtedly leave the
club. Don't you get it!! He's the only hope we've
got.
   Through a series of knee-jerk reactions in an
attempt to play catch-up with the likes of
Arsenal and Chelsea, we are left with a half fit,
unbalanced side, containing a number of big money
misfits, a manager whose future is now in doubt,
a rapidly depreciating share price, and above
all, a chairman who attempts to crash his way out
of his ever continuing cock-ups . . .
   Yours sincerely

 STEVEN HARRIS

➤   At this time, I have to admit to getting a little carried away
over the situation at Spurs. This was because rumours had begun
circulating concerning some fans who had been banned from
White Hart Lane for daring to openly criticise Mr Sugar. Indeed,
some former players were allegedly not being allowed into the
players' bar for an after-match drink. However, with someone as
litigious as Alan Sugar at the helm, one has to be careful about
making unsubstantiated claims. But, there was the question of Bill
Nicholson, the club's greatest ever manager. Initially, rumours
circulated that the board had stopped Mr Nicholson's allocation
of seats in the directors' box. Claude responded accordingly . . .

Tottenham Hotspur

748 High Road, Tottenham, London N17 0AP
Telephone: 0181-365 5000 Fax: 0181-365 5005

Mr Steven Harris

29th December, 1997

Dear Mr Harris,

For your information, Mr Nicholson has retained his
allocation of seats, and is always most welcome.

In view of his fragile state of health, we have
additionally welcomed him as an honorary member of the
Legends Club, and he has availed himself of this
privilege on occasions, as this has the additional
flexibility of being able to sit inside on days which are
too cold to 'brave the elements'.

It never ceases to amaze me at the capacity of a few fans
to invent stories or always seek to believe the worst
without thought or reflection. I know from our previous
correspondence that you fall perfectly into that
category.

Yours sincerely,

Claude Littner
Chief Executive

FOOTBALL & ATHLETIC CO. LTD.
MEMBERS OF FOOTBALL ASSOCIATION AND THE PREMIER LEAGUE

League Champions
1951 1961
League Cup Winners
1971 1973

Winners of the "Double" F.A. Cup and League Championship 1960-61
The European Cup Winners Cup 1962-63 & the U.E.F.A. Cup 1971-72 & 1983-84
Registered Office: 748 High Road, Tottenham, London N17 0AP
Registered Number: 87186 England

Winners of F.A. Cup
1901, 1921, 1961,
1962, 1967, 1981,
1982, 1991

➤   Whilst Claude took the opportunity in this instance to put me firmly in my place, he was providing a continual source of entertainment by at least putting pen to paper. Nevertheless, what transpired from the Bill Nicholson rumours was that the club had in fact withdrawn two complimentary season tickets from the former manager.

In the meantime, following some poor results, there was mounting pressure on manager Christian Gross. And he was about to receive more bad news . . .

CHRISTIAN GROSS revealed he will NOT quit as Tottenham coach despite another setback in his crisis-hit reign.

The Swiss coach's brief period in charge was hit by more turmoil when the Department for Education and Employment threw out a work permit application for his sidekick and favoured fitness instructor Fritz Schmidt.

Harry Harris, *Mirror*, December 30th, 1997

1998

➤   . . . as was our Chairman whose midas touch now seemed to be deserting him.

FOR THE PAST FORTNIGHT, Tottenham's share price has been bumping along the floor at a 12-month low of 75 pence each.

Sugar's stake in the club, worth around £47m last year, is currently worth less than £30m, such has been the depreciation in Tottenham's share value.

Mirror, January 2nd, 1998

➤   In response to his letter of 29th December, I had subsequently discovered that Claude had been unwell. I wrote to him again.

```
January 5, 1998

Claude Littner
Tottenham Hotspur Football Club
748 High Road
London N17 0AP

Dear Mr Littner,
Many thanks for your letter dated 29th December
1997. You are indeed a most entertaining letter
writer.
  I too share your disdain for those people who
invent stories without thought or reflection . . .
  Finally, and most importantly, may I wish you a
full and speedy recovery from your recent
illness.
  I look forward to hearing from you.
  Yours sincerely

  STEVEN HARRIS

PS No photocopied replies please.
```

➤   And I am pleased to report the good news that Claude has
now made a full recovery from his illness.

Spurs 3 – Fulham 1

THE GLORY DAYS are back and the Messiah Jurgen Klinsmann
will lead Spurs all the way back to the Promised Land of
Wembley.

If you believe that, then Christian Gross is a soft touch . . . !

Klinsmann never had a short nor a header of any sort in his
first match against Arsenal, but the German World Cup captain
was presented with five genuine chances against Fulham . . . but
failed to put one away.

Harry Harris, *Mirror*, January 6th, 1998

➤   Harry was still at it, merrily sniping away at Jurgen. But there was some good news. England's left back, Andy Hinchcliffe, was apparently on his way to Spurs.

THE EVERTON MANAGER Howard Kendall yesterday launched a vitriolic attack on Tottenham Hotspur over their handling of Andy Hinchcliffe's proposed move to White Hart Lane. The left-back's £3m switch was called off amid much confusion on Thursday afternoon after Hinchcliffe was told he was not fit enough to complete his transfer.

'The whole affair is beginning to look like a Brian Rix farce,' Kendall said yesterday.

'This is not a case of us being upset because we don't have £3m to spend. This is about a player's future. Having gone so far down the road to signing a player, to then pull out just because he might be unavailable for one game is an absolute nonsense. I feel for the lad. He has been scrupulously honest and then has been treated like this. It's a disgrace.'

Guardian, January 10th, 1998

➤   Oh dear . . . Hinchcliffe was <u>not</u> coming to Spurs. But Italian international Nicola Berti was signed on loan.

Manchester United 2 – Spurs 0

THE PUBLIC RELATIONS hype is over for Jurgen Klinsmann — he owes Spurs a goal.

The German World Cup captain has already collected £100,000 in wages with no return.

But coach Christian Gross fully expects Klinsmann's first goal to arrive against West Ham at White Hart Lane on Saturday.

But as Klinsmann picks up his third wage packet at around £33,000 a week at the age of thirty-three. Tottenham's number 33's time is already up.

Harry Harris, *Mirror*, 11th January, 1998

➤   Change the record, Harry. The attacks on Jurgen were now becoming tedious if not totally predictable. However, he is, it seems, developing some consistency by going through a period of writing absolutely nothing about proposed new signings for Spurs. Which is nice.

Nevertheless, I felt I had to educate Harry concerning his rantings about Jurgen.

January 12, 1998

Harry Harris
The Daily Mirror

BY FAX

Dear Mr Harris,
Whilst you may still be trying to slag off
Klinsmann's form (although it seems stupid to
judge him over just three games) even you were
resigned into admitting that he was the main
reason for Spurs being able to sign Nicola Berti.
I note that in today's article you made
references to the fact that Klinsmann missed six
chances against Fulham. But you need to remember
when you like, because last week you wrote that
he missed 'five genuine chances' (copy attached).
In fact, it was four, and anyone who has the most
limited insight into football could clearly see
that three out of the four were not easy.
  Apart from scuffing one goal attempt, Klinsmann
has hardly had a chance in his two Premiership
games, although he failed to score once in six
chances against Fulham in the FA Cup.
  Klinsmann never had a shot nor a header of any
sort in his first match against Arsenal, but the
German World Cup captain was presented with five
genuine chances against Fulham . . . but failed to
put one away.
  Steffen Iversen has also had to seek medical
treatment elsewhere for an injury (your article -
Spurs in bust-up - 12/1). Perhaps now you'll
write an article about Tony Lanahan's record and
role at the club. You supposedly support Spurs.
Try writing something that may actually benefit
the club.
  Yours sincerely

  STEVEN HARRIS

➤   A trivial point, but Harry must learn.

➤ **15 January 1998** The results of one of football's most notorious investigations, the 'bung' scandal, were released in the British press - one of the main instigators of the inquiry of course being the puritanical Alan Sugar. Harry took it upon himself to outline the facts of how the investigation arose – Harry of course was one of the journalists responsible for unravelling details of the scandal, protraying himself as a champion of good over evil and informing us that 'it was the *Mirror*'s tradition of siding with the little guy that attracted me to work for the paper' (comments noted Harry). No coincidence that the man he directly accused of mishandling club funds was his old adversary Terry Venables. Oh and of course, Alan Sugar was at the time battling to oust El Tel from the White Hart Lane boardroom. It goes without saying that irregularities and wrong-doings must be corrected, and if Harry had information that could lead to guilty parties being apprehended, he was right to inform the authorities and public alike. One final point – the only man in football to have been found guilty of accepting an illegal payment was Arsenal manager George Graham, who was subsequently banished from the game for one year.

BOTTOM OF THE TABLE							
	P	W	D	L	F	A	Pts
Newcastle	21	7	5	9	22	27	26
Sheff Wed	22	7	5	10	34	45	26
South'mptn	22	7	4	11	25	30	25
Wimbledon	21	6	6	9	21	26	24
Everton	22	6	5	11	23	32	23
Coventry	22	5	8	9	21	31	23
Crystal Pal	22	5	8	9	21	31	23
Bolton	22	4	10	8	19	33	22
Tottenham	22	5	5	12	19	39	20
Barnsley	22	5	3	14	19	57	18

26 January 1998 Spurs 1 – Barnsley 1

31 January 1998 Derby 2 – Spurs 1

➤   Meanwhile rumours had been circulating for some months that new investors were interested in taking over at Spurs. According to a financial analyist from a City of London bank, 'predators look at a company that is either underperforming or undervalued'.

THE MIRROR, February 4th, 1998

SUGAR TURNS DOWN £110M BID FOR SPURS

EXCLUSIVE By HARRY HARRIS

ALAN SUGAR has rejected a £110m bid to buy Tottenham Hotspur.

The incredible offer would have landed Sugar, who owns just under 45 per cent of the club, an instant profit of £38m on his £8m investment seven years ago.

Sugar's long-term commitment to the club could not have come at a more critical time.

Spurs face Barnsley in the FA Cup tonight in their last chance to rescue some success from a season that sees them fighting for their Premiership lives.

But Sugar, who believes he can return the club to its former glories, refused to sell.

Tottenham PLC shares have fallen in recent weeks, but at its peak the company was valued at £140m.

Sugar rejected the takeover bid that would have given him a personal profit of £38m.

City analysts have been known for speculating for days that there have been financial predators waiting to pounce on Spurs.

However, those same sources believe that Sugar has become emotionally involved in Tottenham, and that he believes he has a job to do there.

Sugar's commitment to Spurs will be a massive boost to under-siege coach Christian Gross and his players.

➤   Harry informed us that 'Sugar's commitment to Spurs will be a massive boost to Gross and his players.' Really?? On what basis can this outlandishly bold statement be made? Would players who recently were advised by their chairman that 'they were unfit to wear their shirts' celebrate the fact that he was not selling up? And what about the fans?? Would somebody really offer £110m for something which at the time was capitalised at just over £65m, equating to a 70 per cent premium on the existing stock value?

Meanwhile, I still had some previous issues to discuss with Harry concerning the 'bung scandal' . . .

February 4th, 1998

Harry Harris
The Daily Mirror

BY FAX

Dear Mr Harris,
I am intrigued by a couple of your recent articles:
  15/2/96 - Commenting on the Terry Venables case - 'it
was The Mirror's tradition of siding with the little guy
against the money men that attracted me to work for the
paper.'
  4/2/98 - He believes he can return the club to its
former glories. Financial predators have been waiting to
pounce on Spurs. Sugar has become emotionally involved
in Tottenham. He believes he has a job to do there.
Sugar's commitment to Spurs will be a massive boost to
the players. Gross will be given time to pull the club
out from their current free-fall. Gross is gradually
gaining the confidence of his players. A club spokesman
said 'he wishes to keep his head down at the moment'.
  And now the facts:
  15/2/96 - 'I backed Alan Sugar (net worth £150m)
against Terry Venables (net worth £2m).'
  4/2/98 - Financial predators have been waiting to
pounce due to the alarming slide in Spurs' share price
presumably as a result of a series of boardroom
blunders. If he leaves now who's going to employ Little
Daniel? The Hinchcliffe saga once again made Spurs look
like a laughing stock. When has a manager (Howard
Kendall) ever resorted to being so critical about the
unprofessional nature in which an aborted transfer was
handled by the management of another club? The
continuing promises of new important signings, apart
from nine players on loan, have once again failed to
materialise. The full back problem, which yet again
reared its ugly head on Saturday, seems to have been
ignored. Sugar's keeping his head down because
presumably somebody must have finally got it through to
him that his continuing oafish comments were making the
club look even more ridiculous. And finally, why is it
that Spurs have been reduced to sending their injured
players to a foreign country for treatment?
  Perhaps you'd care to comment?
  Yours sincerely

  STEVEN HARRIS

4 February 1998 Spurs lost 3-1 to Barnsley in the FA Cup

TOTTENHAM HOTSPUR shares kicked off at 8.30am when the stock market opened worth 66p and valuing the club at £66.4m.

But they instantly slumped 6.5p – nearly 10 per cent – to 59.5p as dealers woke up to the implications of the FA Cup defeat and Klinsmann's injury. The panic eased by 9am and the shares then bounced back to be 4p down at 62p by 10am.

Then, as news spread that Klinsmann was out for only three weeks, the shares climbed further to be 2.5p down at 63.5p by 1pm.

Harry Harris, *Mirror*, February 6th, 1998

➤   Confirmation that Alan Sugar was still a financial guru. For the record, it was reported that Spurs' greatest rivals Arsenal, the club who for the best part of 100 years stood side by side with Spurs in terms of kudos and status, were now reputedly valued at over £150m.

7 February 1998 Blackburn 0 – Spurs 3

On December 8th, Harry informed us that Christian Gross had 'united the dressing room'. However . . .

DRESSING-ROOM tension is at an all-time high, with squad morale plunging to new depths as the Swiss coach's methods have been dismissed by a host of players at the club. And while his strict disciplinarian regime has not yet driven the players to open revolt, sources at the club have revealed that it might not be far away.

'Things have never been this bad — even when the results were not going well under Gerry,' said a Tottenham insider.

'There is a lack of confidence in Gross. You have to have confidence in the main man.

'He does not have the confidence of the senior players, and when you lose that your position becomes very unstable.'

Mirror, February 9th, 1998

➤   Meanwhile, Harry's pursuit of Klinsmann was relentless.

JURGEN KLINSMANN could be on a collision course with Spurs when he returns to action after breaking his jaw.

The German striker will be pushed to regain his place in the team after a draw against Leicester gave Spurs their best set of results in the Premiership since August.

Certainly it has kick-started a much-needed revival under coach Gross.

Spurs' Swiss coach praised Chris Armstrong for a courageous performance as he lasted the full 90 minutes despite a long injury lay-off.

With Les Ferdinand likely to return soon and David Ginola's best position tucked in behind the front two, there will be fierce competition for places.

Harry Harris, *Mirror*, February 16th, 1998

➤   Harry's upbeat analysis of recent games led us to believe that we should have been dancing in the streets rather than preparing ourselves for a relegation dogfight. In addition, Harry gave us a glimpse of his managerial qualities by suggesting that perhaps Les Ferdinand should play in front of Ginola.

21 February 1998 Sheffield Wednesday 1 – Spurs 0

24 February 1998 Spurs signed Moussa Saib.

Evening Standard

Fans say the 'fat cat' players are overpaid

The table of big chargers for the season 1996/97 is led by Chelsea at £447. Spurs are the only other club to break through the £400 barrier with an average season ticket price of £413. In contrast, champions Manchester United are in seventh place on £330, while the bargain basement belongs to Wimbledon on £152.

➤ Nothing needs to be added. Chelsea challenge for the league and European honours. Spurs fight for their survival in the Premier League.

28 February 1998 Spurs 1 – Bolton 0

➤ There was no stopping Harry on his assault of Jurgen.

JURGEN KLINSMANN'S return to Tottenham is not working out — and that's official.

A detailed analysis of the Germany World Cup captain's 'homecoming' to White Hart Lane by Carling Opta has concluded that Klinsmann is failing to make any impact.

His coach Christian Gross uses the Opta statistics as a guide to his players' performances and the damning evidence is that he has become a £33,000-a-week flop. Klinsmann will lead the Spurs' attack again at Leeds tonight in the absence of the injured Les Ferdinand and Chris Armstrong.

But he is still battling against the pace of the Premiership at the end of his glittering career.

Three years ago Klinsmann was a whirlwind success. Now he is just a shadow of himself, having more influence in the dressing-room than he apparently does on the pitch.

Harry Harris, *Mirror*, March 4th, 1998

```
March 4, 1998

The Editor
The Mirror

BY FAX

Sir,

Yet again Harry Harris seems to be attempting to
undermine the performances of Jurgen Klinsmann at
Spurs (Jur Got To Do A Lot Better), implying that
perhaps Klinsmann should be put out to grass -
after only five Premiership games.
  And yet Mr Harris has never once had the balls
to criticise or undermine the performance of Alan
Sugar - after more than five years.
  Fact - Spurs share price February '97 - £1.40.
Fact - Spurs share price March '98 - £0.68. Fact
- Spurs currently capitalised at £69.4m. Fact -
Arsenal currently capitalised in excess of £150m.
Fact - Spurs involved in a desperate relegation
battle with their third manager in five years, in
what has become yet another 'nothing' season.
  What prospects lie ahead for Spurs?
  The only person who should be put out to grass
is Mr Harris, with his biased, one-sided, and
nonsensical garbage that he continues to spout.

  Yours

  Steven Harris
```

4 March 1998 Leeds 1 – Spurs 0

➤ Matters were reaching crisis point. Spurs had a team in decline, a manager who had seemingly not gained the respect of players (despite some of Harry's earlier articles), and a chairman who seemed to be failing both financially and from a footballing perspective. Despite this, the old Juninho story (rumours that the Brazilian star was unsettled at Athletico Madrid) was up and running again. Of course Harry reminded us back in November '97 that 'Sugar has the financial clout to fund the deal'. This is of course true. But would Alan Sugar part with over £10m to buy one player when the team could conceivably be relegated to the Nationwide League, with dwindling crowds, less TV money, and of course little chance of European football for at least eighteen months?? I don't think so!!

Alan Sugar obviously needed help. It was clear, he was out of his depth, and now presented a pitiful, forlorn figure. Harry was doing his best to rally people into backing the chairman, but seemed to be failing. All along, I had felt that Jurgen Klinsmann was his only shot at retaining Premiership status. Increasingly concerned about Mr Sugar's future, I decided to try and help and launched 'Why Alan Needs Klinsmann After Harry', or W.A.N.K.A.H, and took it upon myself to try and relieve him of his undoubted burden. I wrote to lifelong Spurs fan (at the time worth more than £500m), Mr Robert Earl, who had previously shown interested in buying the club.

March 5, 1998

ATTENTION MR ROBERT EARL

BY FAX

Mr Earl,
I'll lay it on the line!!
Spurs are there for the taking. Not, unfortunately, just on
the pitch, but financially as well.

FACT - Spurs share price February '97 - £1.40
FACT - Spurs share price March '98 - £0.68
FACT - Arsenal currently capitalised in excess of £150m
FACT - Aston Villa currently capitalised at £77m
FACT - Spurs currently capitalised at £69.4m

   Can we really now be worth in the region of £100m less
than Arsenal, even though we continue to fill a ground most
weeks that will ultimately hold 35,000 seats (insulting in
itself that the capacity should be so low)? When Klinsmann
first came to Spurs, you couldn't buy a ticket for love or
money. If Spurs showed ambition, rather than trying to paper
the cracks, or resort to panic buying, the ground would need
to be extended by at least another 10,000 seats.
   Chelsea sign Brian Laudrup, as well as express interest in
Didier Deschamps and Marcel Desailly. And Arsenal make
offers for a £5m player here, and a £10m player there. But
we Spurs fans have been advised that our transfer activity
has ceased for the time being. So we're stuck with the likes
of Steven Carr and Clive Wilson at full back. And if they
get injured, Justin Edinburgh and Dean Austin (presumably
all nice blokes, but not good enough if we want to win
something). Don't get me wrong - most Spurs fans don't
expect irresponsible spending, but there are gaping holes
which need attention. Speculate to accumulate must work,
when top English football clubs are consistently having so
much money thrown at them.
   Alan Sugar has openly blamed everyone from the fans, to
the media, to the players, to the managers. And yet he is
given a holiday by many influential people in the media. The
attitude to fans is 'if you don't like it, lump it!!'.
   I remember some years ago when it was rumoured that you
were interested in buying the club. In view of their
dramatic under achievement over the past five years, Spurs
look like a buy. Don't they?
   Yours

   STEVEN HARRIS

➤   This apathy in responding to my letters seemed to be contagious and unfortunately I didn't hear back from Mr Earl.

JURGEN KLINSMANN has announced he will quit Tottenham after a sensational row with boss Christian Gross.

The pair had a bust-up in the Tunnel after last Sunday's home game against Bolton.

The German captain clashed with Gross over tactics and the role of David Ginola.

He also claimed that Spurs chairman Alan Sugar asked him to contribute his views on team matters when he re-signed for the club in December.

Klinsmann insisted: 'When I came over, one thing Alan Sugar asked me for was my input and that is what I have done, telling Gross and the players what we should change and what we should do better.

'I have put a lot of energy doing that but I have had no feedback. I have reached the point where I have to stop in order to concentrate on my own game.'

Harry Harris, *Mirror*, March 7th, 1998

➤   A sad state of affairs, but who told Klinsmann to 'contribute his views on team matters'?

And now Harry took his chance to go for the jugular.

JURGEN KLINSMANN can leave Spurs immediately if an offer is made for Germany's World Cup captain.

Spurs will consider dumping Klinsmann NOW – rather than wait until his contract runs out in three months time.

Klinsmann is becoming a focal point for unrest in the Spurs dress-room and the north London club cannot afford discord in their fight against relagation.

Harry Harris, *Mirror*, March 11th, 1998

➤ Harry was relentless, and saw his chance to watch Klinsmann fall from grace. Despite this, Klinsmann was asked to intervene. His version of events was highlighted the very next day in the *Guardian*.

JURGEN KLINSMANN'S bust-up with the Tottenham coach Christian Gross erupted after his team-mates asked him to intervene.

'When I was signed by Tottenham I was expected by all sides to take responsibility in the fight against relegation,' the striker told the German magazine Kicker.

'I did that after seeing that many things here [at Tottenham] are in a mess and don't function. There was a lot of tension between the players and the coach. I tried reportedly to be the diplomat and to close the gap. But there was no reaction.'

Klinsmann said his team-mates had asked him to talk to the coach because 'I was the only one who could afford to point out the grievances'.

Guardian, March 12th, 1998

➤ Then this happened . . .

JURGEN KLINSMANN and Christian Gross have dramatically declared peace in their private White Hart Lane war – at least until the end of the season.

The feuding pair have agreed to kiss and make up for the sake of Spurs' Premiership future.

Despite Gross's thinly-veiled threat this week to ignore a clause in Klinsmann's contract and drop the German from today's vital clash with Liverpool, Klinsmann plays — with instructions to haul Spurs clear of the relegation struggle.

It may prove to be a ceasefire at best, but both men are putting on a united front, aware that either or both could be kicked out by chairman Alan Sugar if the insults don't stop.

Mirror, March 14th, 1998

➤ This must have been a major disappointment for Harry. Rumours that he was seen later that night at local nightspot The Coolbury Club, wearing lederhosen, and singing 'Deutschland Deutschland Uber Alles' on the karaoke machine with tears streaming down his face were furiously denied.

Liverpool 3 – Spurs 3

JURGEN KLINSMANN was as good as his word – and showed excellent commitment to Tottenham's cause.

Klinsmann vowed he would do all he can to help Spurs stay up despite his public bust-up with coach Christian Gross.

And Gross hailed the German striker for 'his best game since he rejoined us'.

Of course, that wasn't too difficult to produce after just one goal in nine previous matches.

But Klinsmann's header for Tottenham's opening goal was perfectly executed following a superbly-flighted cross from the right by David Ginola.

Mirror, March 16th, 1998

➤ Aah!! Never mind Harry!! Still, at least you've got an extra chapter to write in the Jurgen Klinsmann biography.

Crystal Palace 1 – Spurs 3

IN A PRIVATE CORNER of Selhurst Park old stone-face himself, Christian Gross, broke into a warm smile.

The Swiss coach had won the battle with Jurgen Klinsmann for control of the Spurs dressing room.

I put it to Gross that the showdown between the two had resulted in Gross taking control and Klinsmann finally producing the goods on the field.

Gross smiled: 'Yes we are all in the same boat.'

And, for a change, pulling in the same director.

Klinsmann's all-round game has risen noticeably and on Saturday it culminated in a world-class finish.

So no more moaning about not getting any chances.

Harry Harris, *Mirror*, March 30th, 1998

➤ Harry came out fighting, and responded by trying to gain some credibility over the whole affair by telling us that 'Gross had won the battle of wills' with Klinsmann. And whilst still trying to throw in the occasional trivial dig at Klinsmann, unfortunately now has no choice but to write positive things about Jurgen's performances.

It seemed strange that whilst Harry may have felt obliged to snap away at Klinsmann, even he must have realised that he was onto a loser when continually trying to back the unfortunate Swiss coach.

➤ Meanwhile, it was heartening to see that Alan Sugar was still throwing his weight around . . .

Marsh drops a TV clanger

RODNEY MARSH was forced into a TV apology for accusing Alan Sugar of being behind the demise of Tottenham for 37 years.

Sky TV's 'Sports Saturday' show was halted for the unprecedented climb-down. Sugar has been at Spurs for seven years.

Marsh unreservedly caved in after his outlandish remarks a week earlier.

Spurs slammed the views of the former England and Manchester City star.

Marsh was put firmly in his place with the climb-down read out on the air: 'We would like to apologise to Alan Sugar and recognise that he had only been chairman since 1991.'

Harry Harris, *Mirror*, April 1st, 1998

4 April 1998 Spurs 1 – Everton 1

➤ Harry outlined a morale boosting victory for the under-fire chairman (above). This is the same chairman who the previous year had the audacity to call the club's fans fickle. And yet, here he was, demanding a formal apology on TV from someone who had made what sounds like a genuine mistake. I therefore decided to address this, and other issues with Harry. After all, I hadn't written to him for over two weeks, and maybe he was missing me?

April 8, 1998

Harry Harris
The Daily Mirror

BY FAX

Dear Mr Harris,
A number of things have become noticeable during the
current football season.

One is that you no longer write about any bogus
transfer signings for Spurs. Is this because you
were found out over the supposed Gazza signing
(13.10.97)?

Another is that whilst you originally criticised
Jurgen Klinsmann's record on the pitch, now you
don't. Is this because a lot of what Klinsmann said
has proved to be true? If he gets decent service,
he'll score, as was perfectly illustrated in the
games against Liverpool and Palace. It seems strange
that you've never made this point.

During the bust-up between Gross and Klinsmann,
where one said he was asked to get involved in team
affairs when he was signed, and the other claimed he
knew nothing about this arrangement – who told one
person one thing, but the other nothing? Who do you
think was the catalyst for such an argument?

It seems obvious that someone somewhere must have
finally told Alan Sugar that he's got to keep his
mouth shut, as well as cutting out all the internal
shenanigans which have caused so many problems and
embarrassment to the club. Everything the man tries
at Spurs seemingly turns to crap. And yet where are
you in all of this? As one of Britain's supposed top
sports journalists, wouldn't it show journalistic
integrity to point out some of Mr Sugar's failings
rather than champion everything he does. Remember,
the share price is less than half than it was
thirteen months ago. Many big money signings have
been flops. And if Spurs do survive, what lies in
store for the team next year? Are we going to have
to play people like Les Ferdinand simply to justify
spunking £6m down the plug hole?

It was particularly eye-catching to see your recent
article in the *Mirror* (Marsh drops a TV clanger –
1.4.98). You specifically pointed out that Marsh was

made to climb down over a comment claiming Sugar had
been behind the demise of Spurs over the last
thirty-seven years, whereas of course Sugar has only
been at Spurs for seven years. But that wasn't the
real point. What Marsh said carried a lot of truth,
even if he got the period wrong. The demise of Spurs
is happening in front of our very eyes. Surely as a
Spurs fan, you must see that. And yet all you can do
is defend one of the main causes.

Your biased, inaccurate journalism makes great copy
for the likes of the Spurs fanzine, but it simply
re-inforces fans' opinions about Sugar, yourself,
and many other aspects of what is so blatantly wrong
about football at the present time.

Yours sincerely

STEVEN HARRIS

11 April 1998 Chelsea 2 – Spurs 0

13 April 1998 Spurs 1 – Coventry 1

April 14th, 1998

THE DROP ZONE

BOTTOM OF THE PREMIERSHIP

	P	W	D	L	F	A	Pts
Wim'don	33	10	11	12	31	34	41
Sheff W	34	11	8	15	48	61	41
Newcastle	33	10	9	14	31	39	39
Everton	34	9	11	14	38	47	38
Tottenham	34	9	9	16	34	52	36
Bolton	34	7	13	14	31	53	34
Barnsley	34	10	4	20	36	76	34
Crystal P	33	6	8	19	28	59	26

TOTTENHAM have joined Manchester United in the race for PSV Eindhoven's £12m rated defender Jaap Stam.

Harry Harris, *Mirror*, April 17th, 1998

➤   Alan Sugar recently went on record to inform suffering fans that the transfer pot was now virtually empty. And yet, here was Harry making a welcoming return to transfer tales with more absolute bollocks.

18 April 1998 Barnsley 1 – Spurs 1

JURGEN KLINSMANN dismissed talk of another rift with Christian Gross last night and revealed that he won't complain if he is axed from Spurs' starting line-up.

Mirror, April 20th, 1998

➤   I just couldn't believe it – all that stuff from Harry about Klinsmann not ever being prepared to be dropped was wrong. Frankly, I was absolutely stunned . . . and of course I had to let his editor know what I thought of the Jaap Stam tale.

```
April 20th, 1998

The Editor
The Daily Mirror

BY FAX:
Sir,
Yet another feeble attempt by Harry Harris to pacify Spurs fans
with the supposed transfer speculation over Jaap Stam. As if
Spurs have any chance of signing such a quality player,
especially after club chairman Alan Sugar recently went on
record to state that little money remained to sign new players
in the foreseeable future.
  Is Mr Harris still trying to protect his good friend Mr Sugar?
Yet again, this story will fail to materialise.
Yours


STEVEN HARRIS
```

REBEL TOTTENHAM FANS last night blasted the club's relegation plight as 'pitiful' – and accused chairman Alan Sugar of
presiding over 'several years of neglect.'

'We are struggling, while Wimbledon are secure again and it
is very disappointing. 'The pitiful thing is that we are not even
on the same planet in terms of competing with Arsenal.'

'We should not be in this position, where our last three games
decide whether or not we are relegated. This is the result of
several years' neglect.'

Mirror, April 21st, 1998

➤   Perhaps Rodney Marsh had a point?

25 April 1998 Spurs 2 – Newcastle 0

2 May 1998 Wimbledon 2 – Spurs 6

JURGEN KLINSMANN'S imminent departure will not be
mourned inside White Hart Lane, even though he leaves again
as a conquering hero with the fans.

Four wonderful goals brought Spurs back from the abyss but,
more important for Klinsmann, rescued his credibility within
weeks of the World Cup finals.

It must be unprecedented in football to actually find fault
with someone who has scored four goals — an achievement that
virtually guaranteed Spurs' survival in the Premiership.

Harry Harris, *Mirror*, May 4th, 1998

➤   Klinsmann scored four goals, and Spurs stayed up . . . and
yet Harry was still gunning for him. Why? And yes Harry, it is
'unprecedented in football journalism to actually find fault with
someone who has scored four goals'. Still, yet more ground-
breaking journalism from White Hart Lane's version of John
Pilger.

Harry went on to excite fans in preparation for the following season with the tantalising suggestion that . . . 'Spurs now need to hold their nerve and maybe Gross is the man to challenge Arsene Wenger . . . ' the question is at what Harry . . . perhaps Boules (*merde*) ??

May 5th, 1998

Harry Harris
The Mirror

BY FAX

Dear Mr Harris,
4.5.98 – another article trying to divert flak from those who thoroughly deserve to be given scathing criticism for yet another shambolic season at White Hart Lane. Rather than continuing to cowardly hide behind the power of your own pen and avoid answering questions over the last year, perhaps you may for once care to deal with the facts:

(i) Jurgen Klinsmann's scoring record is eight goals in seventeen games. Why have you never highlighted Les Ferdinand's scoring record since he has been at Spurs on a four-year contract, earning circa £20,000 per week?

(ii) Did Christian Gross make the decision to sign Klinsmann on a contract which states that the player could not be dropped? Or was this contract authorised by Alan Sugar?

(iii) You have written, 'Spurs now need to hold their nerve and maybe Gross is the man to challenge Wenger. Spurs need a period of stability and it took Alex Ferguson four years to get it right, and the United board retained their patience'. Presumably you are, on behalf of Sugar, preparing us for the fact that Mr Gross, a man whom every football expert has suggested is completely out of his depth, will be remaining at Spurs for another season. As if we will be challenging Arsenal – if Spurs gain a UEFA Cup place next year, Sugar will try and convince everyone that we're a success. Meanwhile, Arsenal will be playing in the Champions League. Spurs fans have been more than patient with Sugar – much longer than four years.

(iv) A number of high quality players are currently available including Deschamps, Kluivert, Desailley, Toricelli, and Weah. Through your supposed network of contacts, which players of note are we really going to sign? (But please please spare us the 'terminological inexactitudes' that you've continually spilled throughout this season.
    Yours

STEVEN HARRIS

JURGEN KLINSMANN has cleaned up with a £250,000 cash bonus for helping to keep Spurs in the Premiership.

I can reveal the amazing level of Klinsmann's supplementary payment written into his contract.

It means the German superstar picked up more than £750,000 in total for just six months' work. With him scoring eight goals in 17 games that works out at almost £94,000 for each goal.

Klinsmann was actually paid closer to £20,000 a week than the reputed £30,000-plus – but his salary was directly linked to Spurs' survival.

Harry Harris, *Mirror*, May 6th, 1998

➤   Another surprise. Harry now told us that Jurgen was paid nearer to £20,000 per week, rather 'than the reputed £30,000 plus'. But Harry, you were the one who gave us that figure in the first place!!

Klinsmann assisted Spurs in preserving Premiership status, which meant that Spurs would continue to fill their ground for at least half of their home games the following season, thus generating millions of pounds. Would this have happened in the Nationwide League? Congratulations must therefore surely go to Mr Sugar for yet another *volte face* when re-signing Jurgen.

Klinsmann subsequently responded to some of his critics. For the record, he scored eight goals in seventeen games. Les Ferdinand has to date currently scored just ten goals in over fifty-five games.

JURGEN KLINSMANN believes that his second spell at Tottenham has been a big success.

The German striker plays his last match for Spurs at home to Southampton tomorrow.

But despite a poor goal return and wages of £25,000 a

week, he believes he has played a vital role in saving the club from relegation and has been excellent value for money.

Klinsmann has scored eight goals in seventeen matches, four of them against Wimbledon last Saturday.

Mirror, May 9th, 1998

9 May 1998 Spurs 1 – Southampton 1

➤ So Klinsmann said 'goodbye' to Spurs. The debate will continue as to whether his second term at Spurs represented good value. But Spurs did survive in the Premier League. And that was presumably what he was brought back to achieve. But what about all the rumblings with manager Christian Gross? Before leaving England, Jurgen appeared on the BBC TV programme, *On Side*. When asked about his time at Spurs, he replied, 'When I got service I scored some goals . . . I don't think I could ever go back to Spurs . . . too much happened . . . alot of people were involved in what happened during the last two months . . . people stayed quiet and I had to take the blame . . . a lot of people knew exactly what was happening and going on . . . '

Whoever could he mean?

Chapter 3

Dear Alan and Harry

Spurs fans left for the summer break confident that if, as was rumoured, a number of high-quality signings were made, the club could be on the way to restoring at least some of its lost credibility. Things began well with fans being suitably rewarded for supporting the club through some very lean times . . .

TOTTENHAM'S long-suffering supporters are to pay the price for the club's Premiership survival with steep increases in the cost of their season tickets.

Standard Sport can reveal they are facing price rises of up to 12 per cent and the scrapping of concessions for children in most areas of White Hart Lane as the club attempts to claw back some of the cash they splashed out on saving their Premiership skins last term.

Evening Standard, May 19th, 1998

➤ Can mere survival in the Premier League justify such increases?

Meanwhile Harry began the summer with yet another blunder. It was comforting to know that in an increasingly unstable world, there are at least some things you can rely on . . .

CHRISTIAN GROSS last night made his first summer signing — and he brought a German back to White Hart Lane.

Tottenham clinched the signature of Borussia Dortmund's twenty-nine-year-old left-back Knut Reinhardt.

Harry Harris, *Mirror*, May 30th, 1998

➤   Then there was more good news for the fans – survival in the Premiership had in fact resulted in a 20 per cent hike in season ticket prices.

THE MIRROR, June 3rd, 1998

PREMIERSHIP PRICE HIKES

Aston Villa	22%
Nottm Forest	21%
Tottenham	20%
Wimbledon	20%
West Ham	20%
Blackburn	15.6%
Arsenal	15%
Chelsea	15%
Middlesbrough	13%
Leicester	11.5%
Coventry	10%
Southampton	10%
Liverpool	10%
Leeds	9%
Sheffield Wed	7%
Manchester United	5.25%
Newcastle Utd	5%
Everton	3.65%
Derby County	0%
Charlton Athletic	0%

➤   The start of the transfer merry-go-round began with rumours circulating in the press that Spurs were trying to sign Patrick Kluivert.

ALAN SUGAR last night publicly declared that Sol Campbell is not for sale at any price.

  Sugar said: 'I am seriously considering asking Richard Branson to release a CD or a top recording so I don't have to keep singing the same song whenever I am asked whether Sol will be sold.'

                                  Harry Harris, *Mirror*, July 18th, 1998

➤   'At any price' — comments noted Mr Sugar.

24 July 1998 Press rumours now circulated that Spurs were interested in signing Jari Litmanen.

26 July 1998 Rumours now circulated that Spurs were trying to sign the De Boer brothers.

29 July 1998 Rumours circulated that Spurs were trying to sign Wim Jonk.

As ever, rumours persisted, but no players were actually signed. And in an article entitled 'Hammers Capital gains', the West Ham chairman Peter Storrie commented, 'I do believe we are now bigger than Spurs', making the point that his club and not Spurs were the third biggest club in London behind Arsenal and Chelsea.

  I wondered how Claude now viewed the situation . . .

July 31st, 1998

Claude Littner
THFC
748 High Road
Tottenham
London
N17 0AP

Dear Mr Littner,
I appreciate how busy you must be with the advent of
the new season, however I wonder if you would care
to comment on the following articles that have
appeared in today's Mirror.

Of course, we must never believe everything we
read in the newspapers, but these stories seem to
have 'done the rounds' in the English press. My
questions are:

(i) Is Sol Campbell remaining as a Spurs player
for the 97/98 [sic] season and not just 'the
beginning' as Christian Gross has apparently
quoted?

(ii) Have Spurs really made any attempts to sign
Kluivert, the De Boers, and Litmannaen? Or are we
just out of our depth?

(iii) Have you seen what West Ham are saying?
(Hammers' Capital Gains – 31/7).

I look forward to hearing from you.

Yours sincerely

STEVEN HARRIS

➤ Soon, as a result of the lack of transfer activity, Christian
Gross had to come clean.

SPURS last night faced up to the bitter truth that they are also-rans in the transfer market.

Boss Christian Gross said: 'We can't make big signings because we're not in Europe.'

His confession came as he unveiled his latest target — little-known Iranian right-winger Mehdi Mahdavikia, 20.

They also have obscure French-Algerian striker Toto Camara on trial from Marseilles at the moment and he will play in tomorrow's friendly at QPR.

That news will dismay fans who are hoping for big-name arrivals to match deals like Manchester United's proposed capture of Patrick Kluivert and Chelsea's early-summer swoops for World Cup hero Marcel Desailly. Danish star Brian Laudrup and Pierluigi Casiraghi.

And Gross piled on the misery by making it clear there will be no headline-grabbing transfers in the near future.

Their only firm signing this close season has been the £1.35m recruitment of left-back Paolo Tramezzani from Piacenza of Italy.

Mirror, July 31st, 1998

➤ It was pitiful. I genuinely felt sorry for Christian Gross. It seemed inevitable that the club were lurching towards yet another crisis. As for Harry, he had been especially quiet recently. Perhaps he had taken a well-earned break, but I thought I'd touch base with him.

```
July 31st, 1998

Harry Harris (Sports Reporter of the Year)
The Mirror

BY FAX

Dear Harry,
The absence of your incisive comment leading up
to the football season has been noticeable
amongst football fans (particularly Spurs fans),
and is of course being sorely missed.
  Are you still writing for The Mirror?
  Yours

  STEVEN HARRIS
```

2 August 1998 Rumours now circulated that Spurs were trying to sign Dwight Yorke.

4 August 1998 Rumours circulated that Spurs were trying to sign Juninho (again).

ANGRY TOTTENHAM FANS are fed up with the failure to sign top-class players.

A Tottenham Action Group spokesman said: 'It is a farce that we have been linked with so many world-class players and come nowhere near to signing any of them.'

Mirror, August 6th, 1998

12 August 1998 Rumours circulated that Spurs were now interested in Matthew Le Tissier.

➤ Harry then took it upon himself to provide news that would warm the cockles of every Spurs fan.

CHAIRMAN ALAN SUGAR moved yesterday to ensure Spurs set the pace in the digital TV revolution.

The club announced the appointment of broadcasting mogul Sam Chisholm as a non-executive director of their plc.

Harry Harris, *Mirror*, August 12th, 1998

➤ Just what we all needed to know as another crisis loomed. 'Spurs set the pace in the digital TV revolution', wrote Harry, but he forgot to inform us that we couldn't buy any players!! He also forgot to tell us that Sam Chisolm, former chief executive of SKY TV, was about to be appointed as a special adviser to the Premier League, which presumably would have created a conflict of interest when the contract for live football rights was to be sold to one of the TV companies.

Pressure was growing on Spurs and their beleaguered manager and chairman. Despite criticism about the problems Spurs were having, Christian Gross retained a dignified silence. Alan Sugar, on the other hand, responded in typically robust fashion.

SPURS CHAIRMAN ALAN SUGAR last night started legal proceedings against David Mellor, head of the Government Task Force on Football.

The club instructed leading lawyers Herbert Smith to act over Mellor's criticism of Spurs manager Christian Gross.

A Spurs spokesman said: 'We are fed up with the constant jibing from someone who is well known as a Chelsea supporter. David Mellor is a failed politician who knows nothing about football and it's about time that somebody buttoned his lip. He should put a shirt on it and a sock on his toes!'

Harry Harris, *Mirror*, August 12th, 1998

➤ Well that's told him Alan!! Mystified by this riposte from our chairman, I sought further clarification . . .

August 12, 1998

Claude Littner
THFC
748 High Road
London
N17 0AP

Dear Mr Littner,
I read an article in today's Mirror, written by Mr
Harry Harris, concerning the issuing of legal
proceedings by Alan Sugar against David Mellor,
over Mellor's criticism of Christian Gross.

According to the article, Mr Harris quoted a Spurs
spokesman as saying, 'We are fed up with the
constant gibing from someone who is well known as a
Chelsea supporter. David Mellor is a failed
politician who knows nothing about football and
it's about time somebody buttoned his lip. He
should put a shirt on it and a sock on his toes!'
Apparently Mellor attacked Gross as the reason
behind Spurs' failure to lure any top class players
to the club. Presumably Mellor is being sued for
libellous comment.

I'm afraid that I do not understand the bit about
shirts and socks, but could you perhaps explain the
real reasons why Messrs Kluivert and De Boer (x2)
failed to sign for Tottenham?

Is the enclosed extract from The Guardian also
considered libellous? Perhaps you would care to
comment.

Yours sincerely,

STEVEN HARRIS

➤   The extract from the *Guardian* referred to the fact that
Gary Brady an extremely promising under-21 midfielder, had
signed for Newcastle on a free transfer, after an 'administrative
error' at Spurs.

➤   The opening day of the season arrived. Spurs had been linked with numerous world class players, but had signed none. How had this happened? It seemed that there were two possible scenarios. Either the public were being misled. Or it was like asking Kate Moss to model Top Shop dresses instead of Versace. Whereas eight to ten years ago Spurs could compete with the likes of Barcelona for players like Patrick Kluivert, nowadays it doesn't matter how much money is reputedly offered, Kluivert too would always opt for the Versace dress.

Spurs took the field on the opening day of the season against Wimbledon. They lost 3-1.

16 August 1998 Now rumours circulated in the press that Spurs were to sign Nwanko Kanu.

More and more people were becoming increasingly concerned at the lack of signings, and obviously attempting to pinpoint the problem.

TOTTENHAM are sensationally set to sue White Hart Lane legend Alan Mullery because he dared to criticise them for not signing new players.

Spurs acted after Mullery rubbished the club's claims that the only reason they have not been able to attract the big names is because they are not in Europe next season.

Mullery, who spent seven and a half years at White Hart Lane making 312 League appearances, last night expressed his 'shock and disbelief' at the club's legal move.

He stormed: 'It's quite likely that Alan Sugar doesn't even know I played for Tottenham'.

News of the World, August 16th, 1998

➤   Sugar once again showed how the democratic process works at Spurs.

DAVID PLEAT yesterday claimed previous Spurs managers had wasted millions on second-rate players.

Spurs have splashed out £30m in the last four years, but Director of Football Pleat revealed that from now on they will only sign top-quality stars.

And Pleat said that if it took £20m to re-build the team, then chairman Alan Sugar would authorise it.

                              Harry Harris, *Mirror*, August 20th, 1998

➤   The old £20m line was dusted down and wheeled out yet again . . . this time by David Pleat, with of course adequate support from the ever faithful Mr H.

And of course I had to ask Harry for his comments (or lack of them) . . .

```
August 20th, 1998

The Sports Editor
The Mirror

BY FAX

Dear sir,
The articles from Harry Harris continue to be so blatantly
predictable. (Bosses wasted millions - Pleat - 20/8/98).
  Here we are, one week into the football season, with Spurs Chairman
Alan Sugar once again on the back foot due to the precarious situation
at the club. Mr Harris seems to be attempting to appease the situation
at Tottenham by producing some half-baked analysis, supposedly from
David Pleat, of the club's transfer spending over the last four years.
This article is a complete fallacy. Does it have something to do with
the fact that Spurs play their first home league game this Saturday?
Many fans are extremely angry with the continuing decline of the team,
especially in view of last week's debacle against Wimbledon. Would Mr
Harris be so kind as to itemise the £40m spent, as well as perhaps
list the players sold during that period, and for how much? People
would then be able to see the net figure spent.
  Pleat insists that the club have pursued a list of world-class
stars. It is easy to make offers for things that are quite simply
unobtainable. I could do it. Surely Mr Harris should outline the
reasons why these players have refused to come to Spurs, and how the
name Tottenham Hotspur FC has deteriorated in status over the last
seven years.
  Yours faithfully

  STEVEN HARRIS
```

MANCHESTER UNITED last night sold Ole Gunnar Solskjaer to Spurs for £5.5m – against the player's wishes.

Although the Norwegian international had told Alex Ferguson he did not want to go, a deal was struck.

Harry Harris, *Mirror*, August 22nd, 1998

➤   Sorry Harry, wrong again!!

22 August 1998 Spurs 0 – Sheffield Wednesday 3

FURIOUS SPURS FANS called for the head of chairman Alan Sugar, claiming he was killing their beloved club.

Mass demonstrations followed this 3:0 home defeat, under-lining the growing crisis at the club just two games into the new season.

Over 1,000 convened shortly after another dire Tottenham display, and refused to move.

For over an hour, chants of 'Sack the board' rang out around the club.

Sunday Mirror, August 23rd, 1998

TOTTENHAM CHAIRMAN ALAN SUGAR last night let rip at the club's angry fans with a four-letter outburst.

Sugar hit out as fans demonstrated outside White Hart Lane after the club's humiliating 3-0 home defeat by Sheffield Wednesday.

More than 1,000 fans blocked the main entrance.

Amid total mayhem more than a hundred stewards, police and security officers were called to the front gate as disillu-sioned fans sat down in defiance, refusing to move and allowing nobody to leave.

Sugar remained inside the ground, and was clearly shaken by the angry demonstrations against him and his board.

Sunday Mirror, August 23rd, 1998

➤   **23 August 1998** Yesterday was hopeful. Obviously, it wasn't pleasant to once again see the team struggling. But I had come to the conclusion that things may well have to get worse before they got better. There was a particularly poignant moment during the game as one fan ran on to the pitch, sat down directly in front of the directors' box, and began gesticulating, pointing an accusatory finger directly at Sugar. Eventually, he was removed from the pitch, to rapturous applause. But I couldn't help feeling a real sense of satisfaction knowing that Sugar was sitting in his seat squirming, exposed to 35,000 people baying for his head. Finally, Sugar may have realised that he had a part to play in the demise of this once great club.

The next day, Harry hit us with one of his exclusives . . .

ALAN SUGAR has been driven to the point where he will decide this week whether to sell Tottenham.

The White Hart Lane chairman was targeted by irate fans after the 3-0 home defeat against Sheffield Wednesday.

Now, I understand, he could hand over control of the club to a suitable new owner following a depressing weekend.

Sugar has grown sick of the personal abuse and the boo-boys who are attacking players such as Swiss defender Ramon Vega.

He was ashen-faced on Saturday as he marched into the Spurs dressing room during half time — something he has never done in his eight years as owner.

Following a poor first-half display, it would not have been a surprise if it was to read the riot act to boss Christian Gross or half the team.

But although Sugar was seething with the performance, he had more pressing matters to deal with. His mission was to console Vega.

The chairman was spotted putting his arm around the centre-half and patting him on the back.

Sugar was concerned for the psychological welfare of Vega following an endless barracking from his own fans.

But Sugar then found himself the victim of hatred as fans protested outside the main gate. The noisy band did not realise the destructive effect their actions were having.

While they were chanting 'Sugar Out', he was trying to negotiate with the agent of Ole Gunnar Solskjaer.

Harry Harris, *Mirror*, August 24th, 1998

➤ This was classic Harry. The story should, as per the headline, focus on how Sugar will finally be selling and the reasons why. But for some reason Harry seemed to prattle on, attempting to portray Sugar as some sort of caring, father figure . . . 'his mission at was to console Vega'. Oh so now we get it. We've got it all wrong. As the half-time whistle blew, Alan Sugar must have brushed aside anyone who came within spitting distance with the immortal words, 'I can't stop now. I must go and console Ramon'. Harry even had the cheek to imply that Spurs fans demonstrating outside the ground, shouting for Sugar's head, could have been the reason for Ole Gunnar Solskjaer not signing for Spurs. Next thing Harry will be telling us that Sugar can't run Spurs because he's gone on a pilgrimage with a party of lepers to Lourdes!!

More rumours continued – this time it was Gareth Southgate.

Soon, potential buyers of Spurs began to be named . . .

BILLIONAIRE BUSINESSMAN JOE LEWIS last night emerged as
the favourite to buy Spurs from Alan Sugar.

But the *Mirror's* exclusive revelation yesterday that Sugar is
now ready to sell has sparked a fascinating race for one of
football's most prestigious clubs. Lewis, 61, was ranked as
Britain's third richest man in 1997, but he faces strong competition from a rival consortium, including the likes of media giant
Rupert Murdoch.

> Harry Harris, Chief Football Writer and
> Anil Bhoyrul, Asst Editor (Business), *Mirror*,
> August 25th, 1998

➤   It was clear, if Sugar wanted to sell, there were plenty of
buyers. I couldn't help thinking that Harry was trying to get
across the 'better the devil you know . . . ' theory to Spurs fans.
There was no question that Murdoch and Sugar were close. But
was Murdoch really ever likely to launch a bid for Spurs in view
of his rumoured interest in Manchester United? Even Murdoch
can't buy two clubs.

However, journalist and lifelong Spurs fan Richard Littlejohn
was another potential bidder, and had expressed interest in
acquiring Sugar's shareholding on behalf of a group of wealthy
Spurs supporters.

On the same day, the *Guardian* ran a story which highlighted
some of the most poignant moments of Sugar's trying tenure at
White Hart Lane, including his quote after sacking Terry
Venables: 'I have done the right thing for the club but will I ever
be able to show my face here again?'. They also pointed out that
following the previous Saturday's defeat against Sheffield
Wednesday, he had invested £50m on players, and £30m on
redeveloping the ground – in addition to telling demonstrating
fans and press alike to 'fuck off'. The article outlined Sugar's
numerous U-turns, and some of his most passionate responses

to his critics: 'I've had enough. I'm serious about selling up. I've worked my nuts off for Tottenham and what do I get? Abuse from these rat-bags, who can all get stuffed', referring to the time when a couple of Spurs fans had expressed dismay to him in the car park at White Hart Lane about the way he was running the club. And of course, one of his earliest soundbites: 'Don't they realise that if I didn't come along, there would now be a Tesco superstore on White Hart Lane?'. The article once again illustrated Sugar's one-sided interpretation of events, but ultimately showed him to be what he is . . . a man who continually seemed to delude himself and who needed some guidance on recognising what it was to make a pig's ear of a situation. And as a consequence, I felt compelled to stick my oar in.

Letters page of the *Guardian*, 27 August 1998

Spurs fans air frustration over Sugar's bitter pill

ALAN Sugar may have invested £50m on players (A crisis too far for would be saviour of White Hart Lane, August 25), but Spurs have also sold nearly £20m worth of players in the same period. And the £30m on redeveloping White Hart Lane has presumably been supported by funds from the Football Trust.

Sugar failed to grasp the concept of investing in football. David Dein, John Hall and even Ken Bates, realised that initially speculating to accumulate was the way forward. Sugar's attempt to defy this most basic of business principles eventually resulted in him buying when the market was at its peak.

Now, the brand name that is Tottenham Hotspur FC has reached such a low ebb that quality players no longer seem interested in joining the club.

The booing and hounding of Sugar has been the result of five years of pent-up frustration. It seems incredible how tolerant people have been. To blame fans for being fickle is ridiculous. He hasn't only messed up on the pitch. One only has to look at the slide in the share price over the past 18 months. He has criticised everyone from players, previous managers, the press, and the fans for the predicament at the club. Take a look in the mirror, Mr Sugar.

Steven Harris
London

➤   Meanwhile, Harry gave it to us straight . . .

THE MIRROR, August, 26th, 1998

SPURS WANT HODDLE BACK

Harry Harris, *Mirror*, August 26 1998

➤   Spurs legend Steve Perryman was asked to assess the situation at Spurs, and proved that it wasn't just 'a few whingers in the crowd' who had a problem with Sugar.

THERE WAS DEEP SYMPATHY for the coach Christian Gross and a shared sense of anguish with the supporters. But surprise at what was happening? None whatsoever.

For Perryman, the fresh-faced lad who arrived at White Hart Lane as a 15-year-old apprentice and dedicated 27 years to Tottenham, there has mostly been wariness over Sugar.

'When I left, part of me felt as if a dagger had been plunged into my heart,' he said. 'But another part felt mildly pleased because I could see the football side being eroded.

'There seemed to be a conscious effort to undermine the power of the manager, and I believe, for successful teams, you need the manager to be a powerful voice.

'It was apparent that in an Alan Sugar regime he didn't want the team boss to be the No. 1 man.'

'Ossie called it the impossible job,' Perryman said. 'You couldn't criticise Sugar's ability to make a pound! But whatever his track record in business he wasn't a football man.'

'When we took over at the club, 80 per cent of fans wished Terry Venables had stayed and not Alan Sugar. By now that affair should be history and Alan Sugar should have become more aware of the football side. But . . . '

Guardian, August 29th, 1998

Saturday 29 August 1998 Everton 0 – Spurs 1

➤   Even with the club in total disarray, Harry put a smile back on everyone's face with a welcome return to new transfer speculation.

THE MIRROR, September 1st, 1998

Spurs line up triple swoop

By HARRY HARRIS

CRISIS club Spurs could have three new faces for their next game against Blackburn on September 9 — and two of them could be from Ewood Park.

They are on the verge of signing midfielder Tim Sherwood for £3.25m and are also chasing striker Chris Sutton in a double raid on Blackburn.

Target number three is Wimbledon defender Chris Perry. Tottenham director of football David Pleat watched the £4m-rated star at Selhurst Park on Saturday .

Blackburn captain Sherwood wants to return to the South and Spurs hope to complete a deal this week.

They would also splash a club-record £9m to land Sutton. It is unlikely that manager Roy Hodgson would sanction the departure of two of his key players. But one or even both of the Blackburn players might favour a switch to Spurs.

➤ Two out of three – not bad for Harry, remarkable even when you consider that both Perry and Sherwood were eventually signed by present Tottenham manager, George Graham, but who was at the time manager of Leeds United. How Harry was able to predict these signings a full year before they took place no doubt prompted the totally scurrilous rumours that Harry was soon to sign on as a palm reader with one of the nation's leading circus acts.

Whilst Harry still kept blanking me, as of course did Sugar, Claude showed that he wasn't prepared to join them in their silence and responded to an earlier letter of mine.

Tottenham
Hotspur

748 High Road, Tottenham, London N17 0AP
Telephone: 0181-365 5000 Fax: 0181-365 5005

Mr Steven Harris

2ⁿᵈ September, 1998

Dear Mr Harris,

I acknowledge receipt of your letters dated 31ˢᵗ July and 12ᵗʰ August.

I am responding in your order.

(i)   Sol Campbell has a number of years unexpired on his contract, and has expressed a desire to
        remain with Spurs, and we most definitely want to retain him. We have developed Sol since
        he was a boy, and he is demonstrating his loyalty to us, which is rare in football today. After
        his wonderful World Cup performance, it was natural that there would be press speculation,
        and enquiries from other Clubs

(ii)   Yes we made an offer for Kluivert, which was accepted by his Club. Unfortunately, the
        player did not appear serious about coming to England, and it came as no surprise that he then
        also rejected Arsenal and Man U.. With regard to the De Boers, we recognised a conflict was
        in progress between the players and their Club, so speculatively we made an approach which
        in the event, and not unsurprisingly, was rejected by their Club.

(iii)   Talk is cheap. West Ham are a 'small' club by THFC standards, but it has to be said that for
        the first time in years and years, they do appear to have a pretty good side.

With regard to the David Mellor comments, I hope you will agree that the man was way out of line,
and appears to be abusing his position. I do not fully understand the shirt and socks comment, and do
not feel inclined to speculate as to the meaning.

Finally, with regard to the Guardian article, the departure of Garry Brady was in my view a shame, as
he appeared t me to be a very promising young prospect. It would appear, however, that in David
Pleat's far more experienced view, the player had an over-rated notion of his worth, and David was not
prepared to meet the players wage demand. I do not therefore accept that his departure was an
'administrative error'.

Yours sincerely,

Claude Littner
CHIEF EXECUTIVE

FOOTBALL & ATHLETIC CO. LTD.
MEMBERS OF FOOTBALL ASSOCIATION AND THE PREMIER LEAGUE

➤   I had just digested Claude's comments about Sol, and
then the following article appeared. Even now, there are still
rumours that Sol and Sugar don't exactly see eye to eye.

SOL CAMPBELL aims to win every top honour in football. Sadly,
he knows he might have to quit Spurs to do it.

Campbell's ambition is likely to force him out of White Hart
Lane unless Tottenham can recover from their latest crisis.

Campbell, who wins his 21st cap tonight, said: "Three years
ago Spurs were a good team. The Ossie Ardiles side and then a
bit of Gerry Francis. But we did not build on it. It was allowed to
fall apart. We have some good players at Spurs, but it is about
chemistry and balance.

'Other clubs are spending money and building. I look at other
clubs with their players and success and it hurts me. I feel I am
getting left behind.

'It is up to the chairman and manager to build a team.'

Sun, September 5th, 1998

➤   Meanwhile, the inevitable happened and Christian Gross
was sacked.

And the rumours continued about who the new boss would
be. Harry gave us an outline of the overall situation.

FURIOUS SPURS FANS are trying to scupper plans to recruit
George Graham as manager.

They are upset that the former Arsenal boss is on the short-
list to succeed Christian Gross, who was sacked at the
weekend. Alan Sugar listened to the supporters when he
decided to put the club up for sale and get rid of Gross.

Now the fans are ready to protest against Graham being
brought to White Hart Lane.

Glenn Hoddle is the crowd's clear favourite after the club

missed out on Ruud Gullit — now at Newcastle. Graham is still resented for his close ties with Arsenal, where he was both player and manager until being sacked for taking a bung.

'I would rather we spent the money on a top-class player than on bringing in Graham.'

Leeds are also doing their best to stop the deal by slapping a £6m ransom on Graham's head. Chairman Peter Ridsdale last night insisted Spurs would not be given permission to talk to their manager.

And in a timely sweetener. Leeds are to release £10m for Graham to spend this autumn.

Ridsdale has put up three obstacles if Spurs refuse to give up the ghost on bringing Graham back to the capital.

A special clause in the 52-year-old Scot's contract states than any club wishing to talk to him must pay a £1m release fee.

Then they must pay up Graham's three-year contracts worth nearly £5m.

And Ridsdale will invoke Premier League rules which forbid clubs to approach managers already under contract.

Harry Harris, *Mirror*, September 8th, 1998

➤   So Harry was telling us that as well as Spurs fans not wanting Graham, after apparently 'missing out on Ruud Gullit' (news to me!!), Leeds were adamant they would not let Graham go and had a number of obstacles to deter any potential predators. So it seemed clear – according to Harry, Leeds wanted to keep George Graham.

In response to Claude's letter dated 2.9.98 . . .

September 8, 1998

Claude Littner
THFC
748 High Road
London
N17 0AP

Dear Mr Littner,
Many thanks for your most informative letter dated 2nd
September, which fortuitously arrived the day before the
enclosed article appeared in The Sun.
   Let's hope that the next appointment of head coach
finally dissuades Sol Campbell from seeking to ply his
trade elsewhere!!
   Yours sincerely

   STEVEN HARRIS

September 8, 1998

The Sports Editor
The Mirror

BY FAX

Sir,
How the hell can Harry Harris have any conception of who
Spurs fans would like as their new head coach (George Is Not
Boss We Want - 8/9). The man has absolutely no idea about
how real fans have felt over the past few years, with his
insistence on writing blatantly supportive articles in
favour of the hateful Alan Sugar. Suddenly, Mr Harris has
become the people's spokesman, telling us that 'the crowd's
clear favourite' is none other than failed England writer/
manager Glenn Hoddle. I, and many others, think not!!
   The supposed £6m ransom money that Leeds may demand to
release George Graham would surely have been better spent by
paying Ruud Gullit a salary over a four year period. Yet
again Spurs have missed out on a golden opportunity, and
Harry Harris has attempted to influence people's thoughts
with yet another 'pie in the sky' story.
   Yours sincerely

   STEVEN HARRIS

➤   David Pleat took temporary charge of team affairs.

10 September 1998 Spurs 2 – Blackburn 1

THE MIRROR, September 12th, 1998 – Harry Harris

SUGAR WANTS £200 M TO SELL

ALAN SUGAR yesterday turned down £80m for Spurs from investment company ENIC.

He believes the club is grossly undervalued after the £623m sale of Manchester United. Spurs might be worth closer to £200m. The explosion of takeover interest has also seen Arsenal valued at half the figure United sold for.

Within two weeks of Sugar making it clear he would sell, he now feels the club has jumped in value.

➤   Surprise surprise!! Sugar said he was going to do something . . . and then didn't. Presumably, he thought that if SKY were going to succeed in their bid to buy Manchester United, (remember Harry gave us all that tosh about SKY/Murdoch being a bidder for Spurs), then rival media companies may enter the scramble to acquire other football clubs. The reason – media companies taking financial stakes or even owning a high profile football club, and subsequently showing live football, could lead to a boost in ratings, even leading to, dare I say it, pay-per-view TV, and, as a result, significantly greater income for football clubs. Never mind the fact that football fans would have yet another additional cost to pay whether they wished to watch their team live, or on TV.

Meanwhile, rumours began circulating about who the new manager of Spurs would be . . . Ruud Gullit, Glenn Hoddle, George Graham, Raddy Antic, even Alex Ferguson. Yeah right, Alex Ferguson is bound to give up managing one of the biggest and most succesful club sides in the world to come and manage a club run by Alan Sugar. Surely it's like asking Bill Gates to take a job at Amstrad?

13 September 1998 Spurs 0 – Middlesborough 3

➤   Harry then told us the fans wanted Hoddle. And then he made us sit up and take note of another potential signing.

TOTTENHAM are ready to make a £5m swoop for England midfielder David Batty.

Following the failure to land Tim Sherwood from Blackburn Rovers with a £3m bid, the north London club has now switched its sights to the fiery international.

Spurs have the money available and are desperate to land a big name signing following another poor start to a season. But new Newcastle boss Ruud Gullit is resisting pressures to sell.

Harry Harris, *Mirror*, September 19th, 1998

➤   Wrong again Harry!!

19 September 1998 Southampton 1 – Spurs 1

➤   The George Graham story gathered pace . . .

TOTTENHAM suffered a double blow yesterday when they were refused permission to approach either George Graham or Glenn Hoddle to be their new manager.

Spurs would face a massive £10m bill if they tried to prise Graham away from Leeds United.

The price of landing Graham would be staggering. A clause inserted in Graham's Elland Road contract, at the request of the manager, demands that any club pays £1m just for permission to talk to him.

Leeds chairman Peter Ridsdale confirmed that Spurs faxed a request to talk to Graham last week, which was immediately turned down by the United board.

Mirror, September 21st, 1998

➤ Apparently Spurs would have to pay £10m for George Graham's services. But Leeds would fight to keep him.

22 September 1998 Harry told us, 'Leeds will hit Graham with a High court writ if he quits the Yorkshire club', subsequently banning Graham from taking up a coaching position elsewhere. Remember, Leeds were adamant that they were not going to let Graham leave.

23 September 1998 Spurs 3 – Brentford 2 (Worthington Cup)

➤ Harry set out the <u>facts</u> concerning George Graham ' . . . he will NOT quit Elland Road . . . '

Graham put the ball firmly in Sugar's court by telling the League Managers Association that he will NOT quit Elland Road . . .

Harry Harris, *Mirror*, September 23rd, 1998

➤ Harry now set out the <u>facts</u> concerning George
Graham . . . he will quit Elland Road.

GEORGE GRAHAM has secretly agreed to take the Spurs job –
and will be the most-hated man at White Hart Lane on Saturday.

He will be despised by Leeds fans for quitting Elland Road,
and not all Spurs supporters are in favour of his imminent
appointment.

Last night some fans chanted 'stand up if you hate George
Graham' during Tottenham's 3-2 Worthington Cup win over
Brentford.

Harry Harris, *Mirror*, September 24th, 1998

Shock of all shocks!! George Graham became manager of
Spurs. Spurs paid Leeds compensation reputed to be between
£2m and £3m and Leeds did not issue a High Court writ against
George Graham. So Spurs employed an ex Arsenal player, and
their most succesful manager ever, a man linked forever in the
minds of most Spurs fans with their hated rivals. Nevertheless,
George Graham's record as a manager spoke for itself, although
there must have been an element of doubt about someone's
allegiance to your team when they reputedly had the crest of
your greatest rivals scribed into the patio of their garden. However, the main issue once again must surely have been about
Sugar preaching one thing, but doing another. Presumably,
Graham forgot about Sugar's acerbic comments regarding his
ignominious departure from Arsenal. I, on the other hand, had
suffered no such memory loss . . .

September 24, 1998

The Editor
The Mirror

Sir,
The most outrageous aspect of Spurs appointing
George Graham as their new manager is the sheer
hypocrisy of Alan Sugar employing a man who was
found guilty of accepting an illegal payment from
a football agent. Sugar constantly reminded us
all about the sleaze running through the game
during the 'bung' scandal constantly attempting
to paint himself as 'whiter than white'.
  What is even more galling is the fact that
journalist Harry Harris, who recently wrote so
passionately about how football continues to lose
all remnants of integrity (ref: Sky's purchase of
Manchester United), doesn't even raise a whimper
when it comes to criticising Sugar about this
scandalous volte-face that he is about to
endorse.
  Yours

  Steven Harris

GEORGE GRAHAM made up his mind three weeks ago to join
Spurs.

I can reveal that Graham has known he would quit Leeds for
some time, and told close friends of his decision.

Now he will finally become Alan Sugar's fifth manager in
seven years after what's sure to be an explosive game against
Leeds at White Hart Lane tomorrow.

Sugar is planning to fly back from a business trip to Los
Angeles to finalise the compensation payment of around £2m
with Leeds chairman Peter Ridsdale.

                    Harry Harris, *Mirror*, September 25th, 1998

➤   Harry now gave us the exclusive about George coming to
Spurs, informing us that Graham had decided to join Spurs
'three weeks ago'. Perhaps Harry should have also apologised for
previously wasting our time, when with his renowned trademark
assurance, he informed us that Graham would be staying at
Leeds. How it is that so many people, with no press connections
whatsoever, and no 'inside track' information, knew that this
was destined to be the outcome of this whole scenario? But the
chief football writer of a national newspaper didn't!!

The hypocritical, even farcical, ways of Alan Sugar were
perfectly set out in the *Mirror*.

THREE YEARS AGO ALAN SUGAR made his views on George
Graham crystal clear.

'If he is guilty, his employer should sack him immediately. If he
were my manager. I would have acted at once — it's taking
money from the club,' he declared.

Arsenal, he said, were 'gutless' and 'had no balls' because
they had failed to deal with the bung scandal which led to
Graham's downfall at Highbury.

How times change, eh?

Sugar, the man who ousted Terry Venables from White Hart
Lane following endless controversy over his 'business dealings',
is now employing the only manager in the game found guilty of
corruption. And what an alliance it promises to be.

This is more astonishing when you remember Sugar's long-
standing feud with Venables.

Mirror, September 25th, 1998

➤   I then received some very exciting news – Harry had
presumably authorised my first letter ever to be published . . . well,
half of it!! (See letter 24.9.98)

Steve Harris, London N4, says: 'It is sheer hypocrisy of Alan Sugar to appoint a man found guilty of accepting an illegal payment.

'Sugar constantly reminded us of the sleaze running through the game during the bung scandal.'

Mirror, September 25th, 1998

➤ Presenting the new £20m line again. Someone please make me eat my words.

GEORGE GRAHAM was told last night he had £20m to make Spurs great again.

Mirror, September 26th, 1998

➤ In view of the fact that Sugar had now increased his asking price to sell the club by over 150 per cent, Richard Littlejohn gave us an uncompromising and brilliantly written summary of his failed proposed takeover bid.

STAND UP IF YOU WANT THE TRUTH, Leeds United supporters aren't the only ones entitled to a full explanation.

For the past few weeks I have remained uncharacteristically quiet on events at White Hart Lane.

That's because I was involved in a consortium attempting to buy a controlling stake in Tottenham Hotspur.

I had no financial interest and no intention of joining the board or taking any part in the management of the club.

The only shares I hold in Spurs are those I was given as a leaving present when I joined the *Sun* from the *Evening Standard* in 1989.

Eighteen months ago Alan Sugar told me on my ITV football show that if he didn't deliver the championship in two years he would stand aside and let 'some other brain surgeon' have a go.

In February this year, when there was the very real possibility of Spurs being relegated. I telephoned Sugar on behalf of a group of wealthy Tottenham supporters to inform him that if he did decide to sell there were people prepared to buy his shareholding.

Over the past few months I have had a number of conversations with him on the subject.

The last time we spoke was after he had announced publicly that he intended to stand down as chairman and sell out.

He told me that he was prepared to listen to offers, but he wanted to be sure any deal would be in the best interests of the club. He also said he wanted his son, Daniel, to remain involved. I agreed to speak to the members of my consortium over the weekend and phone him back to arrange a formal meeting.

On the Sunday, it was revealed that BSkyB had offered £575m, subsequently increased to £625m, for Manchester United.

We concluded that Sugar would probably now revise his valuation of Tottenham but agreed that we would make him a formal offer.

I called Sugar on the Tuesday. He said he would ring back. I rang him a number of times that week. He did not have the courtesy to return my calls. On the Friday I was telephoned by Mihir Bose, a journalist who wrote a brilliant denunciation of Terry Venables, *False Messiah*, with help from Alan Sugar.

He said he heard that I was involved in a consortium to buy the club. I confirmed what he already knew and filled in a few details.

Alan Sugar issued a statement describing the consortium as a 'fantasy.'

I was reliably informed that this was libellous, but since I belong to the sticks-and-stones school I let it pass. Sugar didn't think I was a fantasist when I was writing the truth about Terry Venables and he was ringing me at home to ask my advice.

Richard Littlejohn continued

We made an offer in writing through the Banque Internationale à Luxembourg, where the former Spurs centre half Paul Miller is employed as an adviser. Paul had helped me co-ordinate the bid.

We offered to buy 29.9 per cent of the club at 85p a share. That was a 15 per cent premium above the price quoted on the Stock Exchange that day. We also said we were prepared for Daniel Sugar to continue as director of operations.

It was a friendly offer, tailored to what I believed to be Alan Sugar's aspirations. Our offer valued the club at £85m.

Sugar would have received £25.5m – over three times his original investment – and still retained a ten per cent stake. Some fantasy.

When Mihir Bose telephoned Sugar's press spokesman Nick Hewer he was told in the light of the BSkyB bid for Manchester United, Sugar now valued Spurs at £200m.

In that case, Sugar is stupid as well as greedy. The Stock Exchange still only values Spurs at £74m. But once the Manchester United deal was revealed he reverted to barrow boy mode. In a most astonishing letter to the bank he rejected our approach, adding: 'Mr Littlejohn, as a Tottenham fan, will recall that approximately eight years ago a certain Mr Venables created a swirl amongst the fans against the then chairman Mr Scholar. The general thrust was to intimidate Mr Scholar into selling his shareholding in the club.'

The letter rambled on: 'Unlike Mr Scholar, Mr Littlejohn will realise that my skin is much thicker and my mouth much bigger.' This from the chairman of a public company to the director of a respected international bank. Unbelievable.

Remember, this was a proper approach for shares which Sugar had himself announced were up-for sale. It's a bit like walking into a greengrocer's advertising 'Bananas For Sale',

Richard Littlejohn continued

asking to buy some bananas and being offered a fight by the man behind the counter. Don't you bananas me, mush.

At no stage have I attempted to create a 'swirl' against Alan Sugar. Perhaps it's time I did. Throughout the past few months. I have represented Sugar to my consortium as an honourable man. It is now clear he doesn't understand the meaning of the word. He might have millions in the bank, but he is still two-bob.

If he has something to say to me he can say it to my face, not through the medium of a third party. But like most bullies he is also a coward.

It has become apparent to me that Sugar is a petty, vindictive, little man. Paul Miller has now been refused admission to the players lounge at White Hart Lane and told he is no longer welcome in Legends Club in the East Stand, where former players have always been invited to mingle with fans who pay handsomely for the privilege.

Who has done more for Spurs Paul Miller or Alan Sugar? When was the last time Sugar scored in a European final? Exactly. I have always been grateful to Sugar for rescuing the club from the spivvery of the Terry Venables and Eddie Ashby era. I have defended him in public.

Now Sugar proposes to install as manager Venables' best friend, a man who took a £425,000 bung.

George Graham is fortunate he spent his year in exile on a golf course and not in Ford Open.

Sugar is the man who has posed as the enemy of corruption in football. He was critical of Arsenal for not backing Graham on the spot.

He is also the man who tore up Jurgen Klinsmann's shirt on TV because Klinsmann walked out halfway through a contract. He is now attempting to lure Graham from another club a quarter of the way through his contract.

Richard Littlejohn continued

Sugar is a hypocrite, although he won't acknowledge it. In the late twentieth century, as the Clinton affair proves, life is lived in the present tense. Graham has even convinced himself that he is the victim.

No one is denying Graham's record as a manager. But that is no guarantee. Kenny Dalglish won the double at Liverpool and the league at Blackburn but was a disaster at Newcastle.

The appointment of Graham is a calculated act of defiance. Sugar has a compulsive need to prove that not only is he always right, but everyone else is a complete moron.

The opposite is usually the case.

Graham is a man with a shrine to Arsenal at his home. Spurs fans trying to rationalise the deal should ask themselves this: If Arsene Wenger fell under a bus tomorrow and David Dein rang Graham and said: 'Come home, Georgie boy, all is forgiven,' do you think he would still want to manage Tottenham?

You might also think that if Graham had a shred of decency he might feel obliged to honour his commitment to the club and supporters who rescued him from disgrace and gave him a chance to rebuild his career.

But then, as I have discovered in my dealings with Alan Sugar, decency is in short supply, along with honour and courtesy.

Richard Littlejohn, *Sun*, September 29th, 1998

➤ Harry returned to the fray and wrote a Sugar-friendly piece about how much money George has got to spend, and his new transfer targets . . .

NEW SPURS BOSS GEORGE GRAHAM will head straight back to Leeds in a bid to sign Lucas Radebe and Jimmy Floyd Hasselbaink.

He also wants to bring in his trusted Elland Road assistant

David O'Leary as his second in command at White Hart Lane.

In a move which will anger Leeds fans, Graham has targeted Radebe to shore up his leaking defence and Hasselbaink as a partner up front for Les Ferdinand . . .

Leeds old boy David Batty is a third big-name transfer target for Graham, who has £20m to spend and has already drawn up his dream hit-list.

Spurs chairman Alan Sugar said: 'There has always been money available, it's just that we have not been able to spend it this summer.'

He said: 'You can pay £9m for a player who can then break his leg. So why not pay £3m for a manager?

Harry Harris, *Mirror*, October 2nd, 1998

➤ . . . all of which were wrong. This £20m was beginning to feel like The Holy Grail. We knew it was there somewhere, but nobody had actually seen it.

October 3 1998 Derby 0 – Spurs 1

➤ Even after just one game, George's magic began to work.

A few people had been having a pop at Sugar. And now Teddy Sheringham joined the congregation and came clean about his fallout, giving a detailed insight into how Sugar operates.

NEWS OF THE WORLD, October 4th, 1998

SUGAR MUST GO

TEDDY SHERINGHAM has launched a blistering attack on Spurs chairman Alan Sugar, declaring: Tottenham won't be great again until you GO!

And in an astonishing *Sport of the World* interview, England striker Sheringham warns new White Hart Lane chief George Graham that only bad times lie ahead as long as Sugar in charge.

Sheri whose £3.5m move to Manchester United sparked protests from Spurs fans last summer, said: Spurs will NEVER be great with him as chairman. He has to go before they ever have a chance of hitting the big time again.

Tottenham fans are praying that the arrival of Graham from Leeds last week will finally help them struggling club turn the corner.

But Sheringham warns:

'It might be different with George Graham there, but I doubt it.

'He doesn't know what he is walking into. I'm sure he must have been given certain assurances of how much money he can spend and how much control he will get.

'But he won't have any idea what It is like to deal with someone like Sugar

Pressure

'I can't see George taking any nonsense from above – but I'm sure he will get it from Sugar.

'And, of course, he's a Gooner through and though, If things go wrong, it could start to turn nasty.'

Sheringham reveals today how Sugar helped to drive him out of London. And how the Spurs chairman issued the amazing threat that he would come after him if he ever told his story.

But Sheri added: 'l can remain silent no longer.

'He doesn't want any body to know what goes on at the club. But you can't treat human beings the same as you treat computer chips.'

➤   Teddy went on to describe how Sugar treated him at White Hart Lane. According to Teddy, Sugar said, 'If I see any shit in the papers about me, I'll be after you. I'll hound you down and get my own back'. This, whilst Teddy sat in Martin Edwards' office completing the formalities of his transfer to Manchester United. Teddy went on to inform us that Sugar didn't want anybody to know what went on behind the scenes at Tottenham. How Sugar apparently never listened to an alternative viewpoint (funny that!!). 'He always had to have the last word,' said Teddy. Then Teddy informed us about an incident in which Sugar accused the England forward of feigning injury, and then finally came clean about the transfer negotiations which it appears ultimately led to him seeking a transfer – an initial four-year contract offered by Sugar was subsequently reduced to three. (Further details appear in Teddy's book called *My Autobiography*)

Meanwhile, rumours circulated (this time not from Harry, even after his earlier crystal ball predictions) that Spurs would try and sign Tim Sherwood.

19 October 1998 Leicester 2 – Spurs 1

➤   Sugar soon got more flak in the press. It prompted me to believe that not everyone could be wrong.

O HOW IRONIC that in the week *Titanic* is released on video Spurs release their balance sheet.

Just like that famous ship it showed a massive plunge and a captain announcing that two groups of people should go first. Players and media.

How modest of Alan Sugar to tell the Stock Exchange Spurs made a £1m loss because of 'increased player costs'.

No mention of his own glorious role. How he appointed four managers in the same year that detested rivals Arsenal won the

Double. Might that have affected the financial decisions made by the North London public? Apparently not.

A £7.6m profit was turned into a £1m loss purely because of those greedy young men they call 'players' who hold dear old men like Mr Sugar to ransom.

And as for deficiencies on the management side, dear shareholders, please put that all down to the evil media.

Mr Sugar accepted Gerry Francis's resignation only because our criticism made his job impossible.

And as for Mr Sugar's designated saviour, Christian Gross, that is what he told the City: 'Continued negative media reporting had resulted in a breakdown of confidence throughout the club and the Board had no alternative but to dismiss Christian Gross.'

So there you have it. While football boomed, Tottenham's appalling losses had nothing to do with a dreadful season in which Sugar appointed an unknown Swiss coach who spoke broken English and treated the training group as a concentration camp.

They were rescued by Jurgen Klinsmann — one of those annoying 'players'.

Mirror, October 24th, 1998

```
October 25, 1998

Alan Sugar
THFC
808 High Road
Tottenham
London
N17 OAP

Dear Mr Sugar,
As a shareholder of Tottenham Hotspur plc, it was
disappointing to see that figures recently
announced had shown a previous £7.6m profit
subsequently turned into a £1m loss (1 apologise,
I do not know whether these are annual figures).
I understand that the drastic change in financial
fortunes was as a result of increased player
costs during the 97/98 season, in particular the
signings of Nicola Berti, Jurgen Klinsmann, and
Moussa Saib.
  Saib was signed for a reputed £3.25m. But
Klinsmann and Berti were only signed on loan. I
am assuming that their costs were in the region
of £1m for the season. That still leaves a
deficit of circa £4.5m. Perhaps you could
enlighten me.
  Many thanks.
  Yours sincerely


  STEVEN HARRIS
```

October 27 1998 Northampton Town 1 – Spurs 3

➤ In the past, Harry had told us that 'Sugar had become emotionally involved in Spurs', citing that as one of the main reasons why the dear man had decided not to sell the club. But perhaps there was another reason . . .

ALAN SUGAR, who only two months ago was prepared to sell Tottenham, is seeking the all-clear from the City and shareholders to strengthen his stake in the club.

Tottenham Hotspur plc today made a statement to the Stock Exchange in which Sugar revealed that he would be asking for approval at the AGM on 25 November to buy back shares in the company.

He will also be asking shareholders to approve a waiver he has received from the Takeover Panel that exempts him from making a formal offer for all other Spurs shares he does not own.

In line with many other listed companies Sugar is looking to buy back shares and effectively cancel them in a bid to increase the value of the remaining stock in the company.

But if these shares are bought back it will mean that Sugar's stake in the company will automatically increase. Sugar, through his private company Amshold, currently owns 41.7 per cent of Tottenham and already has a waiver in place from the Takeover Panel that he does not have to bid for the rest of the company.

Standard, November 2nd, 1998

➤   Rupert Murdoch was at the time still trying to buy Manchester United On the back of this deal alone, it was anticipated that a number of football clubs could fall prey to other media conglomerates. If the Manchester United deal went through, shares in these clubs clearly could have rocketed. Spurs had £8m in the bank and this money could have been used to buy a top player, thus increasing the club's success on the pitch, and subsequently resulting in the shares rising. Everyone would gain. But oh no!! Mr Sugar wanted the club to buy its own shares – thus reducing the number of shares in the company, but which would have had the effect of increasing the percentage of shares held by each existing shareholder (ie less shares, greater per-centage). Most Spurs shareholders own just a fraction of 1 per cent of shares. As a result of this financial manoeuvre, their shareholding would increase, but by a nominal amount, adding neglible financial gains to their stakeholding. But Alan Sugar's shareholding would increase by approximately 4 per cent – or by a value of £2.6m if the shares were to remain at their existing price of 64.5p. So if as everyone suspected, the Manchester United deal went through, Spurs' shares could conceivably have 'gone through the roof', and this move would have been seen as a smart piece of business by Mr Sugar . . . or perhaps it could have been construed as buying shares on the cheap.

Remarkably, the Manchester United deal was prevented from going through by Trade and Industry Secretary Steven Byers. Football fans everywhere celebrated – there was a halt (be it temporary) to the game being further sold out. As a consequence of this action, shares in football clubs did not rocket, and media clubs' interest in football clubs cooled – an unfortunate sequence of events for Mr Sugar.

Tottenham Hotspur

748 High Road, Tottenham, London N17 0AP
Telephone: 0181-365 5000 Fax: 0181-365 5005

Our Ref: JS/av(l)702

3 November 1998

Mr Steven Harris

Dear Mr Harris

Thank you for your letter to Mr Sugar of 25 October 1998.

In answer to your query - the increased costs were also the result of player wages -
ie the players you mention and the full year effect of the players bought in the
previous year.

Yours sincerely

John Sedgwick
Finance Director

Tottenham Hotspur plc.
Registered Office: 748 High Road, Tottenham, London N17 0AP
Registered Number: 1706358 England

November 2 1998 Spurs 2 – Charlton 2

➤   A remarkably courteous response from John Sedgwick. Is
there a change of tack from the man at the top even though
he still refuses to personally answer any letters that are sent to
him . . .

7 November 1998 Aston Villa 3 – Spurs 2

9 November 1998 Spurs signed Mauricio Tarricco from Ipswich.

10 November 1998 Liverpool 1 – Spurs 3 (Worthington Cup)

➤   A brilliant result.

12 November 1998 Rumours circulate that Spurs were trying to sign Mark Draper.

14 November 1998 Arsenal 0 – Spurs 0

21 November 1998 Spurs 2 – Notts Forest 0

➤   The Chelsea Ticket Fiasco then came to light . . .

```
November 23, 1998

Alan Sugar
THFC
SOS High Road
Tottenham
London N17 0AP

Dear Mr Sugar,
I am one of those people who wanted tickets for the forthcoming
away game against Chelsea. Is it true that the club were offered
an additional 1600 tickets, but turned them down due to supposed
'lack of demand'?
   Mr Sugar, we are one of the best supported teams in the
Premier League away from home, often filling allocations of
3-5000 when the team plays at Manchester, Liverpool, Tyne and
Wear, & The Midlands. Doesn't it appear that someone may have
got their calculations drastically wrong by refusing an
allocation of just over 3000 tickets for a game which will be
played on the other side of London?
   I sincerely hope that there is not an alternative reason for
this mistake, as some newspapers (with the notable exception of
one chief football writer from a national tabloid) have been
implying over the past couple of days.
   Your comments would be greatly appreciated.
   Yours sincerely


   Steven Harris
```

Tottenham Hotspur

748 High Road, P.O. Box 8445, London N17 0FL
Telephone 0181-365 5050 Fax 0181-365 5101

Ticket Office

Steven Harris

23rd November 1998

Dear Mr. Harris,

I am in receipt of your letter dated the 23rd November 1998 to the Chairman who has asked
me to respond on his behalf.

The Chelsea away ticket allocation was advertised well in advance from Saturday 26th
September with a closing date of Friday 6th November. This was primarily due to the way
Chelsea allocate there away Clubs tickets i.e. in two sections.

The total number of applications received in the 6 week period by Monday 9th November was
1617 applications. This was from both Season Ticket Holders and Members the core
supporters for T.H.F.C.. On Monday 9th November a decision was taken not to take the
second allocation due to the poor response from both Season Ticket Holders and Members.

For information, although T.H.F.C. have a loyal away following a majority do not opt to go to
Stamford Bridge, this has been the case for a number of years now.

Finally, on behalf of the Club I would like to thank you for your continued support.

Yours sincerely

Karen Murphy
Ticket Office Manager

FOOTBALL & ATHLETIC CO. LTD.
MEMBERS OF FOOTBALL ASSOCIATION AND THE PREMIER LEAGUE

League Champions
1951   1961
League Cup Winners
1971   1973

Winners of the "Double" F.A. Cup and League Championship 1960-61
The European Cup Winners Cup 1962-63 & the U.E.F.A. Cup 1971-72 & 1983-84
Registered Office: 748 High Road, Tottenham, London N17 0AP
Registered Number: 57186 England

Winners of F.A. Cup
1901, 1921, 1961,
1962, 1967, 1981,
1982, 1991

➤   – a polite but somewhat distorted letter from Spurs!! What on earth was going on? Where was Claude when you needed him?

Recently appointed Ticket Office manager Karen Murphy attempted to justify the board's decision over the Chelsea tickets. I reminded her about the number of Spurs fans that regularly travelled much greater distances than to Stamford Bridge in order to watch Spurs play. The reason only fifteen hundred tickets were sold the previous year was because that was the allotted amount from Chelsea. In view of the fact that non-season ticket holders find it increasingly difficult to get tickets for the bigger games at White Hart Lane, going to away games can be the only option. I mean, why were the club making such a hoo hah about travelling to Stamford Bridge? What is it that apparently makes it so difficult for Spurs fans to get there? It's not as though one has to negotiate some of the world's most difficult terrain, or fend off any wild animals on route (apart from a few of Chelsea's fans).

There was a school of thought amongst some people (including members of the press) that the reason Spurs didn't want fans travelling to Stamford Bridge was because the game was being shown live at White Hart Lane on the Videotron (a large telly) at a cost of £10 per person. Fans who bought tickets for Stamford Bridge merely put their money into the pocket of Chelsea FC, ie Spurs didn't receive any of the cash!!

Sugar's share-buying proposal was fast approaching, and the board continued to try and defend themselves against the indefensible.

THE MIRROR, November 25th, 1998

BUY STARS NOT SHARES, SUGAR

TOTTENHAM supporters will urge chairman Alan Sugar to make more money available for transfers instead of buying back shares in the club at today's annual meeting.

Some Spurs fans feel the money involved in the buy-back scheme thought to be worth around £8m would be better spent in strengthening the side.

Bernie Kingsley coordinator of the Spurs Independent Supporters' Association and a shareholder himself intends to make his objections known to Sugar.

'Why can't we use the money to buy players or make the ground bigger? It seems to me it's taking money out of the club,' said Kingsley last night.

'Why not add it to the £18m that's supposed to be available and make it £26m?

'You don't get much for your money these days and we need another centre-half, some midfielders and cover at full-back.'

25 November 1998 The Spurs AGM – this was it. I had had enough. I was concerned that I had become this narrow-minded individual who had perhaps become so embroiled in petty trivialities (perhaps this is true), that I no longer saw the bigger picture. Maybe I had got it all wrong about Sugar? Just maybe this dogged, hard-nosed individual would simply overawe those of us who doubted him with his simplistic but brilliant logic, and I would finally understand what exactly he was trying to achieve? After all, I'd never actually met Alan Sugar. Seen how he worked.

I needed to have an open mind and consider everything that was put before me.

And whilst the press were banned from attending, I decided to take down notes of the whole meeting.

Notes of AGM

The formal business of approving accounts, reappointing certain directors and auditors, all took place in fairly quick time. The chairman, Mr Alan Sugar, was questioned about certain issues, particularly, why he had proposed that a dividend of 0.25p per share be paid, when the company's accounts had shown a loss of about £1m. The beneficiaries of such a move are really only the larger shareholders. Most individual shareholders would be rewarded with a negligible financial sum. It was suggested that for the benefit of the company, it may have been better to refrain from paying any dividend, so that the playing staff could perhaps have been strengthened. This is something that all those present at the meeting had agreed 'needed to be done'. This suggestion was dismissed. Alan Sugar is the biggest shareholder at Tottenham.

One of the matters to be dealt with was a proposal by the board which would enable the company to purchase up to £8m of its own shares, thus diluting the total number of shares available, and therefore increasing the percentage of shares held by remaining shareholders. Various questions were asked: 'What was the reason behind the purchase?' 'Will the exercise be repeated in the future?' 'If the company has an £8m cash mountain, why not use the money to buy one, or maybe even two high quality players?' The official line provided by Mr Sugar was, 'Your shareholding will increase. We need this facility in place in case we may at some time in the future need to support the share price, in case of a share price slump.' The principle here appears similar to that of the dividend payment – the major shareholders will be the only real beneficiaries should the share price increase. Most individual shareholders will see their shareholding increase by only a fraction of 1 per cent. This exercise would see Mr Sugar's shareholding increase from 40.44 percent to 44.93 per cent. One man who stood up at the meeting and questioned the motives behind the proposal was answered by Mr Sugar, 'I've already explained it twice. Look, after the meeting I'll write it out specially for you in joined-up writing.' The man concerned had said he had been a supporter for over forty years. Will there be any point in holding future AGMs if Mr Sugar's shareholding increases ever closer to 50 per cent?

Mr Sugar went on record as saying that 'the company needed to speculate to accumulate', an expression previously not shared by former chief executive Claude Littner (see previous correspondence).

Another matter discussed was the refusal of the club to take an additional allocation of 1600 tickets for the forthcoming away game at Chelsea (distance from White Hart Lane – about eight miles). The club were however showing the game live on the videotron screen at White Hart Lane (adult cost – £8). The board commented that the initial allocation of 1400 tickets had been filled, but there was only demand for a further 200 tickets. Board member John Sedgewick commented, 'How do you know whether we'll sell the additional tickets?' This all seems very surprising, bearing in mind that the club regularly fills ticket allocations of between 3–5,000 tickets for games in Birmingham, Manchester, Liverpool and Tyneside. Mr Sugar reiterated, 'There is no hidden agenda here. Chelsea are contravening Premier League regulations by not offering the tickets on a sale or return basis'. Chelsea ticket office commented, 'No comment', over the situation. Could it be that the additional block of tickets offered by Chelsea could not be split in view of potential confrontation between rival fans? Perhaps Chelsea were taking steps to preserve public safety? One man asked, 'Why didn't the tickets go on general sale?'. Board member John Sedgewick retorted, 'They did', only to be corrected thereafter. They did not go on general sale.

Mr Sugar then took it upon himself to attack Mr Mark Jacob of the Tottenham Action Group for stirring up the whole situation, and claiming that a forthcoming TV documentary would be counter productive for the club. When Mr Jacob stood up to respond, Mr Sugar attempted to belittle him in front of the whole audience (Mr Sugar regularly speaks in front of hundreds of people, Mr Jacob presumably does not). Mr Sugar tried to put Mark Jacob on the spot by asking, 'Did you not say that the appointment of George Graham was the final nail in the coffin?' When Mr Jacob tried to deny this (although he actually did make this comment), Mr Sugar asked one of his staff to obtain a copy of the press cutting. Surely Mr Sugar is on dangerous ground concerning comments made in the press: 'If I were Arsenal, I'd have sacked him immediately' (Alan Sugar 1996 – on the George Graham bung saga). Mr Sugar went on to accuse Mr Jacob, as well as Bernie Kingsley from Tottenham Independent Supporters Association, of using the press for their own personal gain, causing a negative aspect of the club. Perhaps Mr Sugar has forgotten his seemingly close association with Harry Harris of the *Mirror*.

Final quote from Sugar:

'As long as I'm chairman, Sol Campbell won't be sold' – 1997.

➤   I'm afraid to say that I was bitterly disappointed. Anyone who dared to question Sugar was simply belittled or humiliated. There was a real sense of intimidation about the place. If Sugar didn't want to answer a question, it was dismissed. I for one wanted to speak up against his rudeness and vulgarity,

particularly about the way he'd spoken to a man who'd supported Spurs for over forty years. People don't need to be
spoken to in such a way. But it was difficult. Alan Sugar no
doubt has become accustomed to speaking in front of large
crowds. I certainly have not. And I regret that at the end of the
day, I had to admit defeat. I am sorry, but this to me was
conclusive evidence that the man was a complete, unadulter-
ated wanker!!

28 November 1998 West Ham 2 – Spurs 1
➤   Spurs lost, but were definitely becoming hard to beat.

The situation about Sam Chisolm becoming a director at Spurs
now came to a head.

**TOTTENHAM are expected to face criticism tomorrow over the
links between the club's non-executive director Sam Chisholm
and the Premier League.**

**Newcastle chief executive Freddie Netcher and a number of
other clubs are understood to be concerned about what they
see as a conflict of interest between Chisholm's role on the
board at Spurs and his recent appointment as a special adviser
to the Premier League.**

Evening Standard, December 2nd, 1998

➤   As a result Mr Chisolm did not taking up his proposed
position with Spurs. The chairman's response in having to climb
down was classic Sugar – illustrating once again how gracious he
could be in defeat. In a statement to the Stock Exchange he said,
'Mr Chisolm will now act as consultant, thereby contributing
exactly the same as he was doing as a director.'

2 December 1998   Spurs 3 – Manchester United 1 (Worthington Cup Quarter Final)

➤   Another great result. Ginola was again outstanding and scored a spectacular goal.

5 December 1998 Spurs 2 – Liverpool 1

12 December 1998 Spurs 2 – Manchester United 2

➤   The good results continued.

22 December 1998 Spurs signed Steffen Freund. Harry was late with the news of an actual transfer happening.

28 December 1998 Spurs 4 – Everton 1

9 January 1999   Sheffield Wednesday 0 – Spurs 0

➤   With Crystal Palace in financial disarray, Harry once again took the opportunity to have a pop at his old adversary Terry Venables. And yet, where was his consistency? If he pleads foul play at one club, surely he's got to do it at every club. And he needed to be told.

January 14, 1999

Harry Harris
The Mirror

BY FAX

Dear Mr Harris
Your rationale over the situation at Crystal
Palace seems to be that Mark Goldberg is dumb and
naive, but the real villain of the piece is . . .
surprise surprise . . . Terry Venables!! And yet Mr
Harris, who ultimately authorises the sale of
players? Is it the chairman or the manager? What
is quite clear is that Crystal Palace have spent
nowhere near £10m.
It's the same old biased piffle that you churned
out about Spurs over the last couple of years,
until such time as you seem to make such an arse
of yourself, that now you rarely write about the
club. Goldberg certainly appears a little naive.
But the same cannot be said of Spurs chairman
Alan Sugar who manipulated boardroom voting
rights to remove Venables in the first place, who
blatantly manipulated the decision to award live
football coverage to SKY (that's the parent
company of your big rivals, in case you weren't
aware), and who now employs a manager whom he
wanted permanently removed from the game less
than two years ago. Your rationale seems to have
deserted you over these issues.
  By the way, who says Venables wasn't successful
at Spurs? They won the FA Cup in 1991. The year
before Sugar arrived. What's happened since then?
  Yours sincerely

  Steven Harris

➤   The saga of matches against Wimbledon began.

16 January 1999 Spurs 0 – Wimbledon 0

**23 January 1999 Wimbledon 1 – Spurs 1
(FA Cup 4th round)**

**27 January 1999 Spurs 0 – Wimbledon 0
(Worthington Cup semi-final 1st leg)**

29 January 1999 Blackburn 1 – Spurs 1

**2 February 1999 Spurs 3 – Wimbledon 0
(FA Cup 4th round replay)**

4 February 1999 Spurs signed Tim Sherwood from Blackburn.

6 February 1999 Spurs 0 – Coventry 0

THE MIRROR, February 11th, 1999

A FLAT BACK FLAW

Wilkinson exposed by slump into Dark Ages

Harry HARRIS
England 0 – France 2

WHAT YOU SOW, you will reap. The men in suits who bowed to the lynch-mob mentality to sacrifice Glenn Hoddle are as responsible as anyone for this debacle at Wembley.

France are world champions, certainly, but England made them look as though they were from another planet.

. . . But going back in time to a flat back four, ditching the modern idea of wing-backs, left England playing jurassic football.

➤   Harry once again dusted off his managerial manual and gave us a fascinating insight into international football tactics . . . I just had to talk to him.

February 11th, 1999

Harry Harris
The Mirror

BY FAX

Harry,
Another intriguing and masterful piece of
journalism in today's paper!!

'The men in suits bowed to the lynch mob
mentality' – presumably you mean the same lynch mob
mentality that prevented the FA from extending
Terry Venables's contract as England manager.
Remember, England managers don't have control over
any transfer kittys. So there wouldn't be any
danger of the odd million quid disappearing, would
there? It is so noticeable how you have never
mentioned that senior players have intimated that
their overwhelming choice to take the job is your
old mucker El Tel.

And now for yet another of your ridiculously
baffling comments, 'Going back in time to a flat
back four, ditching the modern idea of wing backs,
left England playing Jurassic football.' Did you by
any chance notice that France, the current world
champions, played with a 4-4-2 formation?

Forgive my language, but I am afraid to say that
the more articles I read of yours, the clearer it
becomes how much crap you seem to talk.

Yours

STEVEN HARRIS

13 February 1999 Leeds United 1 – Spurs 1
(FA Cup 5th round)

16 February 1999 Wimbledon 0 – Spurs 1
(Worthington Cup semi-final 2nd leg)

➤ A fantastic achievement. In five months George Graham had taken virtually the same group of players that so drastically failed under Christian Gross and moulded a battling, tough-to-beat side that has now reached a cup final.

20 February 1999 Middlesbrough 0 – Spurs 0

➤ Harry quite rightly jumped onto the George Graham bandwagon.

IN A FORTNIGHT of some really remarkable managerial up-heaval at Lancaster Gate, the exploits of George Graham have been generally overlooked.

In any other week Graham would have been setting the agenda by the remarkable way he has turned around Spurs' dismal fortunes.

Such was Sugar's despair at the start of the season that he was on the verge of selling up and getting out. Had ENIC come to the negotiating table with a realistic offer then Sugar would have been tempted to sell.

Harry Harris, *Mirror*, February 22nd, 1999

➤ Harry was doing so well, offering praise where praise was due. And then he went and spoilt everything because ENIC did make an offer that was above the current share price. Isn't that realistic enough?? And so did Richard Littlejohn's consortium. So once again, it seemed Harry was talking nonsense.

23rd February 1999

Harry Harris
The Mirror

BY FAX

Dear Mr Harris,
George Graham has done remarkably well for Spurs in such
a short space of time. Not many people have ever doubted
his ability as a manager. As for integrity, a word so
rare in football these days, his record unfortunately
leaves a lot to be desired.
    As for Sugar, things are a lot more clear cut. His time
at Spurs has been a catalogue of hypocrisy and
contradictions. He was the one who wanted Mr Graham
booted out of football. He doesn't give a toss about
Spurs as a club. All he cares about is boosting his share
price. Why not? He put up the money. But the fact is that
many many Spurs fans told Sugar what he had to do in
order to compete with the likes of Manchester United,
Arsenal, and Chelsea . . . speculate to accumulate!! Bloody
minded as he is, Sugar ignored everyone and dragged the
club into the mire. He thought he knew it all, but was he
wrong? Only last year, having made a complete cunt of not
only himself but the club for the previous five, Sugar
was suddenly heard using the words 'speculate to
accumulate', at last year's AGM. He sat there, with all
his smugness, as though he invented the expression.
Things may be improving on the pitch, but where has
Sugar, the so called financial guru, taken the club
financially? THFC plc is still currently valued at less
than 50 per cent of Arsenal's worth.
    Spurs may win The Worthington Cup this year, but many
fans' celebrations will be tempered by the fact that
Sugar may for some reason be considered a success, when
all he's done, yet again, is bend the rules to suit
himself.
    You championed yourself as a person who sought right
from wrong over the Terry Venables saga. And yet, here
is a person whose chequered history demands
investigation, particularly with regards to his
involvement in football. Are you finally going to be
consistent and do something about it?
    Yours sincerely

    STEVEN HARRIS

➤   Everyone has a tough day from time to time. And this letter is proof. No one can categorically prove that Sugar's only motivation at Spurs is the share price . . . can they??

24 February 1999 Spurs 2 – Leeds 0

➤   Two of the best goals of the season from Anderton and Ginola, who was outstanding.

DAVID GINOLA was last night hailed as the best player in the world by his own footballing hero, Johan Cruyff.
    Dutch master Cruyff puts Ginola ahead of the likes of Ronaldo, Zinedine Zidane, Dennis Bergkamp and George Weah.
                                                    Mirror, February 27th, 1999

➤   Not bad for a Carlos Kickaball!!

27 February 1999 Spurs 1 – Derby 1

2 March 1999 Spurs 3 – Southampton 0

Stuart Houston, George Graham's assistant during his managerial days at Arsenal, was appointed as 1st team coach. And so what of Spurs stalwart, and present coach, Chris Hughton? I thought I'd ask the chairman.

```
March 3, 1999

Alan Sugar
THFC
808 High Road
Tottenham
London
N17 0AD

Dear Mr Sugar,
  I wonder if you could please confirm Chris
Hughton's new role at the club now that Stuart
Houston has been appointed as first team coach,
and also whether or not Chris will have a role
at the club, and in what capacity, next year.
  Congratulations on reaching Wembley.
  Yours sincerely


STEVEN HARRIS
```

➤   No response to this letter.

13 March 1999 Spurs 1 – Aston Villa 0

➤   Harry was soon back with another exclusive – this time he gives us the inside track at what was going on at Manchester United.

THE MIRROR, March 13th, 1999

UNITED DEAL IS FIXED

EXCLUSIVE By HARRY HARRIS

RUPERT MURDOCH has succeeded in his £623m bid for Manchester United.

Mirror Sport can reveal that the Monopolies and Mergers Commission yesterday forwarded their decision to Trade and Industry Secretary Stephen Byers.

The Commission stated there was insufficient evidence to block the BSkyB deal on the grounds that it is anti-competitive.

➤   Sorry H!! You blew it again.

15 March 1998 Tottenham Hotspur plc released their interim financial report. And of course I had to ask about 'the Chairman's Statement' contained in the report . . .

March 16, 1999

Alan Sugar
THFC
808 High Road
Tottenham
London
N17 0AD

Dear Mr Sugar,
I read your statement in the interim report where
you said, 'Consistently competing for honours must
be our objective, enabling us to capitalise on the
riches available to the so called 'big clubs'
through European competition'.
  Do you now recognise that you have been wrong in
the past for criticising fans who begged you to
compete in the transfer market during previous
years, ie to speculate and accumulate (the phrase
you used at the last AGM), so that the club could
benefit from the riches you described above, and
that drawing comparisons with the likes of Wimbledon
(even though they are a wonderful club, but do
survive on a vastly inferior income stream than
Spurs and do not charge some of the highest prices
for season tickets in the country) was also an error
of judgement?
  You see Mr Sugar, whilst we can now all wallow in
the club's recent success, many of us fans were a
little surprised at your interpretation of what a
customer care scheme meant, evidence of which was
adequately provided by former chief executive Claude
Littner when answering questions raised during
previous years. As you are no doubt aware, we, as
fans, will support this club through thick and thin,
and have done so long before you were ever on the
scene, and will unquestionably continue doing so
long after you have gone on to pastures new.
  Your comments would be appreciated.
  Yours sincerely

  STEVEN HARRIS

➤ I can only assume that Sugar must have adopted a new customer care programme by not bothering to ask even Claude or anyone else to respond to any questions.

16 March 1999 Barnsley 0 – Spurs 1
(FA Cup 6th round)

➤ Ginola once again inspired Spurs and scored one of the goals of the season.

21 March 1999 Leicester 0 – Spurs 1
(Worthington Cup Final)

➤ A last minute goal from Alan Neilson after Spurs were reduced to ten men, following Justin Edinburgh's sending off, sealed a memorable victory. The game was no masterpeice, but hopefully Spurs were on the way back.

There were about ten of us who managed to get tickets for the final, fortunately all located in the Spurs end. My friend Darren had a seat in the upper tier, with a decent view but for the fact that one of Wembley's structural posts obscured his vision. As Darren turned his head to survey the overall scene, he couldn't help noticing a man sitting two rows behind him, who presumably also suffered from the obscured view. It was Tottenham's greatest ever manager, Bill Nicholson.

➤ The following day, advice to the chairman this time came not from a fan, or the press, but from the most inspirational player of the season . . . you heard him Sugar.

DAVID GINOLA today challenged Tottenham chairman Alan Sugar to splash out the millions needed to turn the club into title contenders.

The Frenchman helped Spurs to their first trophy in eight years with the 1-0 Worthington Cup triumph over Leicester at

Wembley and then issued his statement of intent to Sugar.

The Spurs side that beat Leicester contained just one new player from the pre-Graham era, Steffen Freund, and with the additional signings of Tim Sherwood and Mauricio Taricco, Graham has spent just £6.5m. When he joined Spurs last year Sugar promised the manager a £20m transfer fund.

Evening Standard, March 22nd, 1999

➤   Harry responded on behalf of Sugar.

ALAN SUGAR will not plough endless pots of money into turning Tottenham into a major force again.

The White Hart Lane chairman once forecast that Spurs would win the League under his ownership and he has never lost the will to bring back the glory, glory days.

But Spurs director of football David Pleat last night warned fans that Sugar would not 'pay crazy money' to achieve that ambition.

And with Spurs in Europe there is every chance of recruiting some of the Continent's top talent.

The Chairman has gained experience from the first few years. Early on he had a few problems not of his making, as there was no one on the board with a football background.

Harry Harris, *Mirror*, March 23rd, 1999

THE MIRROR, March 25th, 1999

I don't smack people in the mouth nowadays but I won't kiss their backsides either.   (Alan Sugar)

➤ A class quote from a class man.

I wondered if Harry had any views about Bill Nicholson's seat at Wembley.

```
March 25th, 1999

Harry Harris
The Mirror

BY FAX

Dear Harry,
 Are you aware that Bill Nicholson, without question the
greatest manager in Spurs' history, and still performing
duties on behalf of the club, was given a 'restricted view'
ticket for last Sunday's Worthington Cup Final?
 Yours sincerely

Steven Harris
```

➤   Obviously not. Despite numerous letters from me, Harry had never responded. Probably too busy digging up 'exclusives'

OLE GUNNER SOLSKJAER has revealed that he turned down a
£1.5m double-your-salary offer to sign for Spurs.

The Manchester United striker was Tottenham's target at the
start of the season.

He earns £850,000 a year at Old Trafford, but the offer from
White Hart Lane would have made him to top earner at the club.
                                Harry Harris, *Mirror*, March 26th, 1999

➤   See what I mean. Another corker from the great man.
Don't Spurs have a wage ceiling of circa £25,000 per week?
That's the reason why Darren Anderton has recently turned
down a new contract, isn't it? So how can they offer more than
circa £30,000 per week to a new player? It doesn't make sense.
Then again . . .

```
March 29th, 1999

Harry Harris
The Mirror

BY FAX

Dear Mr Harris,
You're at it again!! Trying to defend some of your bogus stories.
Ole Snubbed Spurs' Cash - 26/3 - did Spurs really offer Solskjaer
£1.5m a year? Or is this yet another story to try and convince
people that Sugar thinks big when it seems he's just begun to
warn people via David Pleat that 'we will not pay crazy money'.
It's not very convincing telling people 'we offered him this
much', when nothing happens. Anyone can make offers. If you
remember, you've got it completely wrong when writing about
Solskjaer before (copy enclosed - 21st August 1998).
  There's nothing wrong with financial prudence, but
unfortunately Sugar, the so called great financial guru, has been
in charge of the club for over seven years (not 'a few' as Pleat
supposedly said in your article dated 23rd March) and which is
currently worth approximately one third of Arsenal's value.
  According to you, Pleat also said, 'Early on he had a few
problems not of his own making', which is of course absolute
crap.
Yours sincerely

STEVEN HARRIS
```

➤   I had to take up the Bill Nicholson story with Karen
Murphy.

```
 April 1, 1999

Karen Murphy
Ticket Office Manager
THFC
808 High Road
Tottenham
London
N17 0AD

Dear Karen Murphy,
Is it true that Bill Nicholson was given a
'restricted view' seat for the recent
Worthington Cup Final?
  I await your comments.
  Yours sincerely


 STEVEN HARRIS
```

3 April 1999 Spurs 0 – Leicester 2

➤   The build up to the FA Cup semi-final begun with Spurs
having to play a rearranged league game against their semi-final
opponents Newcastle.

5 April 1999 Newcastle 1 – Spurs 1

9 April 1999 Karen Murphy responded to my earlier letter
(1.4.99), this time by phone, informing me that 'Bill Nicholson
was not given a restricted view ticket'.

11 April 1999 Newcastle 2 – Spurs 0
(FA Cup semi-final)

➤   A gallant effort which saw Spurs denied a blatant penalty, but eventually succumbing to Newcastle's firepower up front – something which Spurs unfortunately lacked and which no doubt George Graham will attempt to address.

Harry's journalistic prowess soon suffered a blow.

World Soccer Extract – March 1999

IF ANYBODY SEES HARRY HARRIS, the *Mirror's* Chief Football Writer [*sic*], reading *World Soccer*, could they please relieve him of his copy? Poor little Harry clearly can't be trusted to read the magazine in a responsible, adult manner.

The day before the first leg of Manchester United's Champions League clash with Internazionale, Harris's 'Big Match Preview' featured quotes from a host of Inter players and the then coach, Mircea Lucescu.

It was impressive stuff. Where did Harris get his quotes from? Did he: A) fly out to Milan and interview the players personally at Appiano Gentile, Inter's training ground, B) pay someone else to get the quotes for him, or C) sit on his backside in London, open the March issue of World Soccer and copy our exclusive interviews verbatim, without paying us a penny?

We'll give you a clue: it wasn't A or B.

➤   And again.

GEORGE GRAHAM will attempt to raid former club Leeds to find a goalscorer who can turn Tottenham into a major force next season.

The White Hart Lane manager believes that youngster Alan Smith will fit the bill.

                                Harry Harris, *Mirror*, April 13th, 1999

17 April 1999 Nottingham Forest 0 – Spurs 1

20 April 1999 Charlton 1 – Spurs 4

➤   The true state of affairs concerning the £20m transfer kitty is revealed by George Graham –

GEORGE GRAHAM has revealed that his team rebuilding plans at White Hart Lane are threatened by lack of money.

The Tottenham manager issued a challenge to chairman Alan Sugar after last night's 4-1 win over Charlton at the Valley to provide him with the necessary cash to continue the remarkable revival at White Hart Lane.

Graham said: 'Twenty million? I wish. I don't know where that figure comes from. It is not true | that I have been given that sum to spend. I want new players, at least three of them and I am still I looking at how best to bring them into the club.'

Evening Standard, April 21st, 1999

➤   And of course, I had to let Harry know the news about the manager's comments . . .

```
April 23rd 1999

Harry Harris
The Mirror

BY FAX

Harry,
When George Graham became Spurs manager, you told
readers of the Mirror about the £20m transfer
kitty that Sugar had made available (copy
enclosed). You've written about all these
fantastic players that 'Spurs are looking at'.
And yet, surprise, surprise - what's happened
this week? Graham has said, 'I don't know where
that figure comes from'. Any chance that yet
again Sugar has performed another U turn? Or,
just like previous years, the money was never
there in the first place? I mean, if he can win
trophies with the existing squad, why spend
money? An article investigating what can only be
described as unfounded rumours would be a
worthwhile piece of journalism.
   Finally, have you seen the latest issue of World
Soccer (copy enclosed)?
   Yours kindly


STEVEN HARRIS
```

➤ Remember Harry, £20m means £20m net. Surely we've got to add to our squad – not buy one or two quality players only to see existing quality players sold. Sugar has consistently prophesied about the game getting out of control with ridiculous transfer fees and wage demands, meaning some clubs could go to the wall. He may well prove to be correct in respect of those clubs unable to generate sufficient revenue. But on average, ticket prices at Spurs far exceed those of Wimbledon, even Arsenal. In fact it has been suggested that Spurs' total gate receipts still exceed virtually every other club in the UK (yes even Manchester United and Chelsea). So if he wants to charge Rolls Royce prices, give us a Rolls Royce team.

24 April 1999 Spurs 1 – West Ham 2

➤   And I also wondered what the chairman's view was on the manager's comments.

```
April 26 1999

Alan Sugar
THFC
808 High Road
Tottenham
London
N17 0AD

Dear Mr Sugar,
Rumours are once again rife in some newspapers that the
previously reported £20m transfer kitty available to
George Graham does not exist. In fact, it is reported
that Mr Graham needs to sell players in order to
generate funds for new players. One newspaper has
reported that all funds generated from a recent
sponsorship deal, totalling some £3m, will be made
available. Presumably, there will be other funds added
to this sum.
  So, in order to dispel all of these rumours, could you
clarify exactly how much money, net of transfer sales,
Mr Graham is to be provided with in order to buy new
players?
  Many thanks.
  Yours sincerely


STEVEN HARRIS
```

➤   No response to this letter. But no doubt we'd all be happy if Sugar did 'speculate to accumulate' as per his comments at the recent AGM.

1 May 1999 Liverpool 3 – Spurs 2

5 May 1999 Spurs 1 – Arsenal 3

➤   For those who saw it, this was conclusive evidence that there was still a long way to go.

Congratulations to David Ginola who won the award from both the players and sportswriters and became Player of the Year.

10 May 1999 Spurs 2 – Chelsea 2

DARREN ANDERTON could be on his way out at Spurs after he rejected the same pay packet as David Ginola.

Harry Harris, *Mirror*, May 14th, 1999

➤   A worrying development.

TOTTENHAM STAR ALLAN NIELSEN has slapped in a written transfer request — just two months after being crowned as their Wembley hero.

Mirror, May 15th, 1999

➤   More worrying news, but thankfully Alan Nielsen is staying put for the time being.

16 May 1999   The season ended with Spurs visiting champions elect Manchester United. The scenario was quite simple. If Manchester United won, they were league champions. If Spurs drew or won, the title could go to Spurs' great rivals Arsenal. A difficult scenario for most Spurs fans to stomach – and another battling performance saw Spurs take the lead through Les Ferdinand. However, despite an outstanding performance from goalkeeper Ian Walker, Manchester United came through and won the match 2-1. Nevertheless, from the most turbulent of beginnings, George Graham's team had unquestionably made outstanding progress in just seven months leaving Spurs fans eagerly anticipating the season ahead.

The close season again saw Spurs linked with a number of high quality players. Spurs did sign Chris Perry who appears to be settling in extremely well. Willem Korsten was also signed from Leeds Utd, but has yet to start a game for the first team. In view of the team's lack of firepower up front, it was suggested that one of George Graham's absolute priorities was to sign a new striker. Spurs were linked with Chris Sutton (signed for Chelsea), Emile Heskey, Michael Bridges (signed for Leeds), and Robbie Keane (signed for Coventry). A promising start to the season has subsequently seen fit again striker Les Ferdinand pledge to George Graham, 'Let me save you £8m'. In addition, Harry reported that, 'Spurs offered £7m for Frank Lampard.' This was subsequently denied by West Ham manager Harry Redknapp in the fanzine *Over Land and Sea*, who confirmed, 'Spurs did want to buy him, but they only offered £4.5m'. Spurs also agreed to sign full-back Najuan Grayeb, but for some reason this deal failed to materialise, with Grayeb subsequently signing for Aston Villa but apparently threatening to sue Spurs over the aborted transaction. Spurs did hit the headlines in other ways – cashing season ticket cheques prior to the season starting, but not actually delivering season tickets to fans until after two home matches had been played. Will these people receive a refund Mr Sugar??

Conclusion

On Saturday 21 August 1999 at 5.50 pm, I had a telephone call from my friend John. 'I can't believe it. We're top. It's absolutely fucking brilliant', he screamed, like some excitable kid. Spurs had just defeated Sheffield Wednesday 2-1 at Hillsborough, and for the first time in fifteen years, and for the very first time since the formation of the Premier League, were top of the league. The feeling was, as John had so aptly described, one of disbelief coupled with incredible excitement. There we were, above Manchester United, Chelsea, and yes, Arsenal. Sure, it didn't last. Manchester United went back to the top twenty-four hours later. And although it's early days, congratulations must go to George Graham and the players for what they have achieved in such a short space of time. George Graham may have his doubters, but he is unquestionably an inspirational manager. The improvement in some players' performances, since his arrival at the club, Steven Carr for one, has been truly outstanding. Of course every Spurs fan would love to see exciting, sexy football, and if we were to become 0-0 specialists, it's likely that the doubters would grow. But the fact is that as yet, this hasn't happened. To criticise someone for being boring, after Graham's achievement in such a short period of time, is just downright stupidity.

But I regret however that whilst praise can be heaped upon Mr Graham, I cannot, as some people may think I should, offer Alan Sugar any congratulations whatsoever for employing Mr Graham in the first place. Nor will I ever be able to accept him as chairman of Tottenham Hotspur Football Club. As this book hopefully demonstrates, Sugar is one of those individuals who can never, it seems, accept responsibility when things go wrong. Who thinks that his opinions are the only ones that count. Who so ruthlessly rebukes anyone who doesn't think the Alan Sugar way. The simple fact of the matter is that if Sugar had instructed Claude Littner to respond with just a hint of courtesy to my and other people's letters back in 1996, this book would never have been written. As far as putting information together, Sugar makes it easy, because of the way he often responds to those who may have a different train of thought. He should remember – good manners cost nothing.

But most importantly, Sugar needs to face up to some harsh facts. It's hard to admit, but Spurs are now London's third or fourth club. If any top international players want to come to London, more often than not, the first clubs they'll consider will be either Arsenal or Chelsea. This never was the case before the arrival of Alan Sugar. And yet, he has never once been big enough to acknowledge this fact. Spurs are currently capitalised at between £70m and £80m. Arsenal are reputedly worth as much as £250m, and Chelsea at around £180m. That clearly doesn't show evidence of success, when for over a hundred years, both Spurs and Arsenal stood side by side in terms of kudos and status. In footballing terms, the appointment of George Graham was a good move. But the hypocrisy stinks. Sugar was the most vocal club chairman to denigrate Arsenal for not sacking Graham on the spot over the bung scandal. How can the man have the gall to employ someone he so viciously attacked less than two years later? The PLC may be profitable, but the man clearly has no foresight, because if Spurs as a club can still generate the income that it has done on the back of being also-rans, what sort of income could be generated were the team to be vying for a place in the Champions League? Once again, it has often been mentioned by Sugar friendly-journalists that George Graham was promised £20m to rebuild the team. Graham has often voiced his desires to acquire a quality striker. But yet again, things have gone quiet. If Sugar decides to break the bank because of mounting criticism, it will be a job well done. Remarkably, Spurs are a lot closer to perhaps rejoining the batch of top clubs. But further investment is needed.

There will be no doubting that if Alan Sugar wants to, he will use all the power that he has to try and make a mockery of this book. Yes, Alan Sugar, the man who has consistently held the press responsible (with one notable exception) for many of the problems at Spurs, actually does have some friends in some very high places. This book simply outlines the events of the last three years. Sure, we've got to look forward. But why should someone like Sugar get away with things?

I am not, as Sugar may attempt to say, a doom-monger who wants to cause more problems for the club. Nothing whatsoever could be further from the truth. I have supported Spurs for over thirty years, travelling far and wide, and will continue to support them until my dying day. Believe me, if Sugar ever resigned, it would have no bearing at all on how George Graham and his team perform on the field – as Sugar would obviously like people to think. Remember, Spurs won the FA Cup when they were in dire financial straits. Which leads me onto another thing. Alan Sugar saved Spurs? Sure, he outbid Robert Maxwell to gain control. But it is beyond all comprehension and reasonable commercial sense to think that the group of administrators responsible for deciding Spurs's financial future back in 1991 would ultimately have resolved to close down a club that simply because of its name and heritage, would, and did, attract a number of erstwhile investors, prepared to rescue it from its financial plight. Not as Alan Sugar has ridiculously put it, reduced the site to 'a Tescos supermarket', if he hadn't come along.

And as for Harry, well, I didn't write all those articles. My situation with Harry is similar to that of Sugar. If he hadn't reacted in the way he did at White Hart Lane during the game against Notts Forest (and believe me he did), there probably wouldn't have been a book. But he illustrates so much about what is wrong with football today, arrogantly dismissing anyone who disagrees with him.. This sort of attitude seems rife throughout the game. He is, after all, meant to be a journalist, and one would assume he should portray the thoughts of the public

The fact is that Sugar and Harry are extremely powerful people. Sugar has money, and money gives you power. And as I've said earlier, Sugar has important friends in the press. As for Harry, he writes for a readership of three and half million people every day. His opinions can influence many of those readers, most of whom will read only that paper. But who can dispute it? Sugar and Harry remind me of two know-all, spoilt kids who attempt to bully anyone who gets in their way. And yet, all they seem to do is make themselves look ridiculous and foolish. I genuinely hope that their influence doesn't continue to stultify what could potentially be one of the great football clubs of the twenty-first century.

What Happened Next

You can't write an opinionated book about Alan Sugar and Harry Harris without asking them for their comments. That is to say, in the democracy in which we live, freedom of speech is imperative.

STRICTLY PRIVATE AND CONFIDENTIAL
TO BE OPENED BY ADDRESSEE ONLY
Alan Sugar
Tottenham Hotspur Football Club
748 High Road
Tottenham, London N17   21 October 1999

Dear Mr Sugar
<u>"Dear Alan, Dear Harry"</u>
I act for Steven Harris, who has written a book entitled "Dear Alan, Dear Harry", concerning correspondence that he has had with Tottenham Hotspur Football Club and Harry Harris.

I enclose with this letter a draft of the book.

The purpose of me sending the draft to you is to invite you to put forward any comments that you wish on the material which my client is intending to publish. Although, he is confident of the accuracy of the material published within the book, if you feel that there is anything inaccurate he would be pleased to consider making amendments. Similarly, if there is any general statement that you wish to make, then consideration can the given to having it included in the book.

I look forward to hearing from you within 14 days.

Yours sincerely

David Price   **David Price & Co** Solicitors

And obviously we sent an identical letter to Harry for his comments too.

Four days later, Mr Sugar responded . . .

Tottenham Hotspur

Chairman's Office

Mr David Price
David Price & Co
Solicitors
5 Great James Street
London
WC1N 3DA

Please reply to:-

Brentwood House
169 Kings Road
Brentwood
Essex CM14 4EF

25th October 1999
Your Ref: 421.DP

Dear Mr Price

Thank you for your letter of 22nd October, together with enclosure.

As you will appreciate, all my staff and I are very busy; we do not have any time to read what looks like a very thick document. Your client has not been commissioned by us to write a book about me or Tottenham Hotspur Football Club. It is therefore not our job to edit your client's book or to check its accuracy, this, with all due respect, is something you should be doing. No doubt you will inform him that he needs to take due care and attention.

I would like to make it perfectly clear by way of this letter that in no way or form do I or Tottenham Hotspur Football Club endorse the publication of your client's proposed book. For the aforementioned reasons, in sending it to us inviting us to edit it for him in no way compromises our rights to take whatever action we may feel necessary after publication.

I herewith return the document unread.

Yours sincerely

A M Sugar
CHAIRMAN

Encl.

League Champions
1951 1961

Winners of F.A. Cup
1901, 1981, 1961, 1962,
1967, 1981, 1982, 1991

League Cup Winners
1971 1978 1999

FOOTBALL & ATHLETIC CO.LTD.
MEMBERS OF FOOTBALL ASSOCIATION AND THE PREMIER LEAGUE

Winners of the "Double" F.A. Cup and League Championship 1960-61
The European Cup Winners Cup 1962-63 & the U.E.F.A. Cup 1971-72 & 1983-84
Registered Office: Bill Nicholson Way, 748 High Road, Tottenham, London N17 0AP
Registered Number: 57186 England

sportswear partner

Mr Alan Sugar
Brentwood House
169 Kings Road
Brentwood
Essex CM14 4EF   27 October 1999

Dear Mr Sugar

<u>Dear Alan, Dear Harry</u>

I write further to your letter of 25 October, which was received today.

I was not asking you to edit the book or check its accuracy. This is something that my client has done. Nevertheless, in accordance with normal practice, it was appropriate was to let you have sight of the book in order for you to make any comments. No doubt, if we had not shown you the book, you would have been the first to complain that you had not had an opportunity to comment on its contents.

You are a wealthy individual in charge of a large publicly listed company with access to sophisticated press relations advice. I cannot believe that you are unable to show this relatively short book to one of your PRs for comment. Nevertheless, I note what you say.

Yours sincerely

David Price   **David Price & Co** Solicitors

Meanwhile, Harry was as consistent as ever – we never heard a word from him. The interesting thing about Harry is that over the last year, he has rarely reported on Spurs matches, preferring instead to provide us with his wisdom on the wider issues of football, as well it seems only reporting on matches at Highbury and Stamford Bridge. It does beg the question – does Harry still support Spurs? I sincerely hope he's not one of these people that only supports a team when they are succesful, just like some of us use to do when we were ten. Nevertheless, one thing remains clear. Harry can still manage to create an impression throughout the football world. Just ask West Ham. Recently, Harry unleashed another 'exclusive' concerning a forthcoming book to be written by former West Ham midfielder Eyal Berkovic. 'According to Berkovic, West Ham are a racist club', Harry told us. And what was the outcome of this story that looked set to rock English football? There follows some comments from West Ham's manager Harry Redknapp (courtesy of *Hammers News*) following his team's home win over Bournemouth in the Worthington Cup . . .

'Eyal Berkovic never said what was in the *Mirror*. We've got a copy of his book here, it's been translated and it's not in his book.

'Eyal was distraught, he could not believe what was written.

'The club's racist . . . ? My best mate in the world's a Jewish fella. How can we be racist?

'Eyal never said it anyway and it's a disgrace what Harrv Harris has written and he knows it.

'Harry Harris never interviewed the boy.

'This is the crap we have to put up with now. I think the game's gone with some of the * * * * * that gets written these days.'

And there rests the case for the defence!